To

_____

On the Occasion of

_____

From

_____

THE GARDEN OF GRACE

Treasures from the Golden Book

JILL BRISCOE

MONARCH
BOOKS

Oxford, UK & Grand Rapids, Michigan

Published in association with the literary agency of Alive Communications, Inc.,
7680 Goddard Street, Suite 2000, Colorado Springs, CO 80920, USA.

First published in the UK in 2007 by Monarch Books
(a publishing imprint of Lion Hudson plc),
Mayfield House, 256 Banbury Road, Oxford, OX2 7DH.
Tel: +44 (0) 1865 302750   Fax: +44 (0) 1865 302757
Email: monarch@lionhudson.com   www.lionhudson.com

Distributed by:
UK: Marston Book Services Ltd, PO Box 269, Abingdon, Oxon OX14 4YN.
USA: Kregel Publications, PO Box 2607, Grand Rapids, Michigan 49501.

ISBN: 978-1-85424-766-7 (UK)
ISBN: 978-0-8254-6132-3 (USA)

Photos: Bill Bain, Charles Chouler, Francis Chouler, Roger Chouler, Estelle
Lobban, Caroline Nicholls, Geoff Nobes, Anne Rogers.

British Library Cataloguing Data
A catalogue record for this book is available from the British Library.

Printed and bound in China.

TO STUART,

THE MAN OF MY LIFE: PARTNER IN THIS

GRAND ADVENTURE OF MINISTRY FOR

ALMOST FIVE DECADES, AND WHO, ABOVE

ALL, IS A MAN OF "THE BOOK".

MY "WORDSMITH" WHO HAS TAUGHT ME

HOW TO LOVE, STUDY, APPLY AND TEACH

THE WORDS OF LIFE AND LIGHT.

WHAT JOY! THANK YOU.

CONTENTS

Foreword   10
Introduction   11
An altogether different thing   13
The Golden Book   17

AGEING   20
    Extra time   20

CHRISTMAS   26
    A baby cried and a lion roared   26
    A ministry of presence   31
    Surprise   39
    Victoria   42
    Kneeling with kings   47

COMFORT   49
    Somebody's praying for me   49
    Who put out the stars?   51

DEVOTION   57
    Clear air   57
    A stilling of the soul   60
    The "yes" of the soul   62
    What would Daddy do?   64
    So little redeemed   68
    Come early   73

EASTER   76
    Till I get home one Easter   76
    You wore my thorns   84

FATHERNESS   86
    Father deep   86
    His Father's eyes   90
    The beat of my Father's heart   95

MINISTRY   98
    Friends with Jesus' friends   98
    Harvest time   100
    My uniform   102
    Spent   106

RUNNING ON EMPTY   107
    Flat camels   107
    Coming apart before we come apart   113
    Hanging up your harp on the weeping
        willow tree   116

TRAVEL   122
    Across the miles   122
    The lock box   126

TRIALS   132
    Time   132
    Trials   133

WISDOM   134
    A can of worms   134

WORRY AND FEAR   143
    A gratitude attitude   143
    Heartsick   147
    The thief   152

FOREWORD

*J*ill Briscoe is passionate. She is passionate first and foremost about her communing with the risen Lord Jesus. She allows us right into the heart of her prayer life as she brings her anguish, her doubts, her joys to Him and then finds her perspective transformed. In the harsh realities of life, yet also the wonders of life, Jill centers on what inspires, drives, and enables her – the constant visits and dialogue with her Lord.

Jill is remarkably vulnerable. She rips away the veil of self-deceit and lays bare before the Lord the depths of her own weakness and despair. She truly believes she is a sinner in need of grace – and the joyous reality of this book is that she finds that grace. In these pages she prays, "Ignite my poor faith till it dances in praise."

That's the theme of this book, and the reader enters into the journey that brings on the praiseful dance. When at our Christianity Today board meetings Jill, as a fellow trustee, has led us in extended prayer, we are all thoroughly aware of the spiritual dynamic that permeates the room and our lives. She leads us in prayerful engagement to be instruments of God's peace.

Many thousands of seekers all over the world have listened to Jill pour out her heart and share what the Lord Jesus is doing in her and others' daily experiences. As you read, you too will sense her passion and spiritual vitality.

Harold Myra, Editor in Chief, Christianity Today

INTRODUCTION

*S*OMETHING HAPPENS WHEN your soul sits down and has a rest. It's always quiet on "the Steps", you know. The Steps of your soul; sweetly quiet and the air so still and different from any other place on earth. And joy – a whispering of love that seems to be saying, "I see you. I'm coming." And He always does, because it's His Book, you see. He lives in the words and He knows that if we will only hand over our hearts and lend our minds to the Spirit – and, of course, our wills to obey – He will help us find the Golden Words in the golden hues of the morning in the Golden Book.

Do you have a Golden Book? What colour is your Bible? Did anybody ever tell you that if you take your Book to the Deep Place where nobody goes – in the Garden of Grace – and sit still till He comes, and ask Him, "Open Thou mine eyes that I may behold wonderful things out of Thy Law" – when you open your eyes He will be there and will point out the points and you'll get it! Yes, you will! You'll never want to stop then. But, of course, you'll have to, to eat or sleep, work or play, just for a little while.

It was years ago, when I was just a girl – eighteen years of age – that I met the Author of the Golden Book and, of course, the whole direction of my life changed. Once I became a Christian I was told to read my Bible every day. I started well, but after a bit it became a push to do it. The excitement of my conversion faded and my first love began to grow cold. One day I felt a hunger growing inside. It was as if my soul was reaching out after Him, looking for His smile, the warmth of His arms and the touch of His Spirit that I had experienced when first He called my name.

And I remember… Walking in the English Lake District – Wordsworth country – while attending the Keswick Convention, I found a bubbling stream. I sat on a nearby rock, pulled a New Testament out of my pocket and began to read. When I began, the little red book in my hand was just a little red book. But when I'd finished, the course of my life was set. The secret was mine. The words had become "God's Gold" to me. All that now remained was a lifetime of sitting on the Steps with Him and learning the art of true devotion. Here on these pages are some of the secrets of this art.

It is my heart's deep wish that through this little book I can make you hungry for "God's Gold", too.

Jill Briscoe

AN ALTOGETHER DIFFERENT THING

⎯⎯⎯⎯⎯ ⬿ ⎯⎯⎯⎯⎯

T LAY ON THE STEPS UNOPENED. I'd formed a habit of leaving it by the Front Door so I'd know where to find it quickly. Of course, I had other copies of the Book. They were all over the house in case I happened to have an unexpected minute or two (some hope!) in the middle of a busy day. They were on my bookshelves, in the bedroom, lying open in the study, and there was even one in the kitchen!

These God Books were bound in leather, burgundy, black or a nice deep blue, and they had the same words in them as the one waiting for me on the Steps outside the Front Door. Yet I found out, that when I read them without taking time to sit still in the

Spirit's clear air and asking Him to turn the pages and teach me the truths, it was as though I needn't have bothered reaching for them at all.

It wasn't that a snatched piece of Scripture couldn't help me; but somehow such rushed religiosity didn't shake my soul awake or turn my worldview on its head. A hasty glance at a page of holy writ, with the radio on in the background and my hands full of laundry, was like popping a candy in my mouth – sweet for a moment but soon gone.

I remember the day I realized that this sort of reading didn't heal a wound caused by people who wanted to hurt me, or save me from regrets that haunted my dreams. The quick fix I'd hoped for from the hastily ingested words didn't seem to have the power to chase away a fear that leered around the corner of tomorrow either. And I never got a swift solution to how to tackle a deep and personal dilemma, sing in the rain, shout in the storm, or survive a tsunami! They were wonderful words and I believed them, but they didn't seem to make any lasting difference.

But when I trod quietly in the Garden of Grace where the Steps began and sat down in the misted mysteries of God, and when I just "was" for a time; till I woke up inside to an awareness that He "Is", then I knew something had happened – not only "Heart Deep" inside me, but, strange miracle, to the Book as well – it was "golding". And by the time we got comfortable, He and I, this harried, hurried one, settled in to the Spirit's stunning stillness, I wondered greatly how it was I didn't come here more often – perhaps 40 times a day!

The first time I noticed things were radically different was when I invited Him to read the Book *to me*, instead of me reading it *to Him*. It was then, before my very eyes, the red Bible began to change: it became lighter and more "golden" than ever – an altogether different thing.

"Lord," I remember saying to Him, "When I asked 'You' to read the Golden Book to me it was if I was reading it for the very first time!" He was looking at me very seriously so I knew that this was a very important conversation we were having and no light matter.

In His hands the burgundy copy I had left at the Front Door was steadily growing more "golden" by the moment! And when He opened the Book, it was to a passage I *never* would have thought of reading if I'd been flicking through the pages in haste, trying to "get my devotions done and out of the way"!

And so a habit began. At the end of our misty moments in the dawn on the Steps of my soul, I began to write down some of the points He pointed out to ponder from my ponderings! I wrote them in books and I wrote them in scripts; some found their ways into journals, letters, magazines and emails. I just kept on passing on the wonderful golden words He had given me to my world full of people, some of whom don't even know about the Front Door, the Steps of our soul, God's Gold and the One who loves us to distraction and who waits for us in the Deep

Place where no-body goes.

I have found out that people love to hear the golden words I've gathered, and want to know "where on earth"

I heard them. It's hard to explain I haven't heard them "on earth" at all, but from heaven. They may have never seen a Bible or, like me, have lots of Bibles available, but they don't take "Heart Deep" time with Him. They tell me they read only from Bibles that are black or burgundy or blue, with black print on white pages, and have never in their lives experienced reading from a Golden Book and what that does for your soul!

And so I pray that here and there across the world some people who may have possessed many Bibles all their lives will get excited – like you, my dear reader – and decide to go "Heart Deep" too, sitting still in the "mist of the mysteries" with Him. Whenever you do, I promise you, you will find a miracle happening within you in the Deep Place where nobody goes, and you and your world will surely be the better for it! Then, in a little while, you'll see that your whole life will be transformed into "an altogether different thing"!

THE GOLDEN BOOK

Words of God on golden page,
Words of life that never age,
Touching heart, transforming mind,
Treasure, rich for humankind.
Words of God are mine to read,
Words of God my spirit feed.

Words that teach me righteousness
So, humbled, I my sin confess.
Living words that light my way
Encourage me when low I lay.
Words that comfort all my days,
Words that turn my pain to praise.

Run I to the soul's Deep Place,
Falling prostrate, seek Your face,
Find myself in Your strong arms,
Safe, secure from all that harms.
Word of God a fortress high
Till the trouble passes by.

Words of God I must declare,
Preaching Jesus everywhere.
Golden gifts you are to me –
Gospel, setting people free.
Help me use the Spirit's sword,
Words of God from my great
Lord.

Truth en-fleshed in Christ who came:
O Living Word I praise your Name!

EXTRA TIME

"SINCE MY YOUTH, O GOD, YOU HAVE TAUGHT ME, AND TO
THIS DAY I DECLARE YOUR MARVELLOUS DEEDS. EVEN WHEN I
AM OLD AND GREY, DO NOT FORSAKE ME O GOD, TILL
I DECLARE YOUR POWER TO THE NEXT GENERATION…"
Psalm 71:17–18

I WAS SOMEWHERE IN ASIA. My birthday was coming up.
A rather significant one. There was nothing I could do to stop it
happening! I could wring my hands or stamp my feet, pout or
fume, pray for hours, or even call an all-night prayer meeting
with sympathetic friends in an attempt to stave it off. It would do
no good. It would happen anyway. I even went Heart Deep to
check the dates were right.

"As You said two thousand years ago, Lord, 'Who of you by
worrying can add a single hour to his life?' (Or subtract one!)
There was no heavenly comment so I began to ruminate on the
inevitable. I was going to be seventy years old!

A few years ago I had been speaking at a women's event, and my hostess had left me a basket of fruit and a little note card with a greeting and a verse of Scripture in my room. After reading what was written on the card I went to look in the mirror. Better get a better publicity picture! I thought. The verse was from Psalm 71 in the Golden Book and it read: "Even when I am old and grey, do not forsake me, O God, till I declare Your power to the next generation, your might to all who are to come."

After sitting on the edge of my bed and meditating on the idea, I realized this was more than a kind note from the committee wishing to encourage an ageing warrior who looked a little worse for wear. This was a word from God! I read it from the Golden Book again and this time it looked quite different.

I noted the verse that came before it: "Since my youth, O God, you have taught me, and to this day I declare your marvellous deeds." I remembered my youth and my conversion at college in the UK. Memories of the wonder of discovering Jesus – or, rather, of Jesus discovering me – flooded over me. Pictures of my friends' shocked faces as I struggled to explain whose I was and who I now served danced in my mind. Most of my friends found it impossible to reconcile the new Jill with the old familiar one and left me.

I thought about my rich heritage…John Stott and C. S. Lewis, a professor at Cambridge when I attended college there. I thought of the chance I had had to attend the famous Keswick Convention where I had listened to famous British preachers.

And I played back the memories of being taken along to hear a young and vibrant Billy Graham preach at the now-famous Harringay Arena Crusade in London.

I thought of meeting and marrying the love of my life and fellow "declarer of His might and power", and the ten wonderful years when we left the business world and worked together on the staff at a youth mission, roaming the streets of the UK and talking to kids who had never heard that Jesus was alive and had the power to change their lives as He had ours. And I thanked God all over again for my heritage of life and service.

I thanked God for our three children, all busy declaring His power to their generation, with our grandchildren "in the blocks", getting ready to go. And last but not least, I thanked God for my British roots nurtured in American soil, and the thirty learning and growing years at Elmbrook Church in Milwaukee, Wisconsin. Yes, on that day years ago, the verses from Psalm 71 had walked off the page and into my life, making themselves at home. And I had taken out my Bible and marked the place so I would know where it was when I needed to remember it – like now!

We, my husband Stuart and I, have just been in countries where freedom for the church is curtailed. Sitting on the floor in a hot, humid, upper room with thirty pastors' wives, teaching the letter to the Philippians – God's Gold – I worked hard to explain the 2,000-year-old words of an aged man, restricted in a prison yet declaring His power and might to the next generation of believers – I watched the careful attention and eager note-taking. Some of these women are younger than my own children, I thought. In fact, two of them were the age of our eldest grandchildren!

These servants of Jesus are the next generation who must carry the torch to their children and grandchildren after them. They have no heritage like mine. They have few Bible helps, teachers or even Bibles. Not one of the women had heard of The Beatles or, for that matter, Billy Graham! For them, things are just plain difficult. Yet there is so much joy and laughter. Worship is whispered, prayer intense, hunger for the Word of God evident.

"Don't stop," they asked me wordlessly, after an hour-and-a-half teaching session. What joy to be here. What privilege.

Suddenly the young daughter of one of the pastors' wives

who was playing "lookout" rang a little bell, a warning that the police had come. Everyone flew across the room finding cupboards and drawers to hide their Bibles and notes in. Looking about in panic I saw a cupboard nearby and hid my Golden Book and notes inside. Turning around I found my sweet friends well prepared for the eventuality.

They knew about my birthday and have prepared a special cake. Suddenly, as all the Bibles disappeared, a table appears with a birthday cake, decorated with my name on it. I am gently nudged into the centre of a circle of women and a cake knife is put in my hand. My new friends gather round and offer a hearty rendering of something that sounds vaguely like "Happy Birthday to you". This time the singing is at the top of their voices! The police come and go. They don't bother to look too closely, thank God! One sits down for a minute, his back against the wall, watching. We play party! We celebrate and photos are taken; a little time passes and the men leave. All is peaceful again and they say we can finish Philippians 2! I will not soon forget this birthday!

When the time comes to return to the hotel (we are tourists), a sweet young woman comes to me shyly, struggling with her English. She says, "This last Sunday we honoured our elderly people and we gave them a verse of Scripture to encourage them. I want to encourage you, too. Please come back and finish the lessons from Philippians. We have not had a chance to hear this teaching. This verse is for you from the Lord."

I knew without looking where she had opened her Bible,

before she read in halting English: "Even when she's old and grey, do not forsake her, O God, till she has declared your power to the next generation, your might to all who are to come!" I cried. She cried. We all cried. I promised her that if I possibly could, I would come back another day.

A week later, I was sitting high in the skies flying to New Zealand for more declarations of His power and might – this time to the next generation of Salvation Army officers – and I read my verse again. Suddenly He was right there.

"I told you in my Golden Book that your allotted lifespan is 'three score years and ten', so in one week's time you will have completed it and join your Stuart in 'extra time'!" He said.

"Yes, Lord," I answered, a little apprehensively.

"Remember what your friend, the soccer coach, told you when his matches went into extra time?"

"You mean what he said to his players if they tied a game?"

"Yes."

Remembering, I laughed out loud! "Yes, Lord. He said 'If my players find themselves in extra time I tell them: Take risks and go for goal. Give it all you've got and never give up.'"

He looked at me. I looked at Him.

"OK," I said. "I'll do it!"

"I knew you would," He said.

So that's what my Stuart and I are doing. Hey, it's all right – in fact, it's a grand place to be. Hurry up and join us. The next generation is waiting!

CHRISTMAS

A BABY CRIED AND
A LION ROARED

I RAN TO THE STEPS OF MY SOUL to decorate them. It was Christmas. Usually I put holly around the Front Door (it reminds me of England) and silver bells (they remind me of America) and candles all the way up the Steps of my soul (they remind me of the "Bright Light". You know the one I mean – the Light of the world).

This year I decided to do something different. I went shopping and decorated with lions! There were baby lions and teenage lions and big lions. The thing was, I had been reading in the Golden Book about the Lion of Judah and I realized it was His birthday!

I was just finishing my work and everything looked lovely when I dropped my box of lions. Suddenly He was there helping me to pick them up.

"Nice," He said, smiling and helping me to tidy up. We worked in companionable silence and then sat down for a talk.

He sat there holding a baby lion in His hands. There were deep furrows in His face and deeper thoughts in His eyes and suddenly it didn't feel quite right to be sitting on the same step as He was, so I slipped down a step or two and turned around so He was above me. That felt better, especially when He was sitting there so quietly and thoughtfully with the little lion lying in the palm of His hand. (You know, the palm of His hand with the deep dark places in the middle.)

"You are the King of Israel – Mighty Lion of the tribe of Judah," I murmured.

"You say well."

"I worship You!"

After a little time He left and I stayed a while tidying up the Steps, brushing the stardust around the candles to make little twinkly nests. Then I thought about it all and wrote my thoughts down. I left my poem for Him in the mail box (the silver box by the never-extinguished lamp outside the Front Door. Someone, I don't know who, always collects the mail every day – even on holidays like Christmas!)

My poem was about lions. A baby lion lying in a wooden box made from a tree. Someone made the box, a carpenter, I suppose. Ironic don't you think? Who knew that one day it would hold a baby carpenter?

A silly world passed on by in Bethlehem, except for a few who needed God in the worst way. Needed God deep down in the Deep Place where nobody goes. You know, the poor, the rascals, the camel hands, the foreigners from strange lands with strange tongues; then there was the drunk they threw out of the pub who stumbled in by accident and found a place to sleep – alongside God as it turned out. What did they see? Oh what did they hear that night?

> When you came a baby child,
> Tiny, helpless, meek and mild,
> Did the watchers hear you cry?
> Did they ever wonder why
> When you cried in trough of hay
> It seemed a lion roared that day?

That Christmas, the wonder of our conversation kept coming back to me and I spent a lot of time on the Steps of my soul reading the Golden Book and enjoying my decorations and the talk we had. And each time I added a bit more to my poem and posted it in the silver box.

> The baby cried and the stars grew dim,
> The angels wanted to rescue Him,
> Then donkeys knelt and the Father smiled
> With a heart of love for the baby child.

The baby slept in the warm embrace
Of a teenage girl with a tear-stained face.
The girl was thin and the man was poor
And some shepherds stood at the stable door.

The baby grew up so the world could be saved
Through His death on a cross and His empty grave.
Then the angels fell down to love and adore
And heaven fell silent when Judah's Lion roared!

THE GARDEN OF GRACE

Lord God help me to understand the height, the depth, the width of Your love. How could it be that the Mighty Lion of the tribe of Judah became a child? And for me, reduce me to size, show me Your mercy. I kneel at Your crib in worship!

Amen and Amen

A MINISTRY OF PRESENCE

" '…THEY WILL CALL HIM IMMANUEL –
WHICH MEANS, 'GOD WITH US.'"
Matthew 1:23b

───────────── ⌒◯⌒ ─────────────

*J*ESUS DIDN'T DO MINISTRY from a distance. He didn't send an angel to redeem the race. He came – IMMANUEL – God with us.

"Our God contracted in a span – incomprehensibly made man."★

"God was reconciling the world to Himself in Christ."★★

"I just had to come," He said. And He came. Our ministry has to be the same. A ministry of presence. I went to the Steps of my soul to talk to talk to Him about it.

The Golden Book was lying by the Front Door. There was the most wonderful fragrance, so I looked around to see where it was coming from and I saw it came from some beautiful flowers.

─────────────────

★ Charles Wesley.
★★ 2 Corinthians 5:19.

They must have grown up overnight; I hadn't seen them there the day before.

"Christmas roses," He said, coming to sit beside me.

"They're lovely, Lord," I said plucking one. "Thank You for planting them! They remind me a bit of a carnation."

"Incarnation," He said briefly. "I'm glad you like them." Then, "Don't let Me disturb you – read My Book." He handed me the Golden Pages and I settled down, ever so aware of His sweet company.

It was quiet, so quiet. I read for a while. The words said: "As the Father has sent Me, I am sending you". I glanced at Him to see if He had seen where I was reading from, but He seemed to be thoroughly occupied with some heavenly thought, so I hastily turned the page. I had been baulking about going on a mission trip I had been asked to lead and the verse was a little disturbing to say the least!

Serbia and Croatia were at war and I was joining a delegation from the charity World Relief (I was on the board) to go and see what the churches in America could do to help thousands of refugees pouring over the border. They also wanted me to

speak in some of the churches to encourage believers in the region. But it was a really inconvenient time (war is never convenient) and I had a dozen good family reasons to say "no" to this trip.

I noticed the Christmas roses smiled as He put His hand on my arm and asked me if I understood what I was reading. What did those beautiful flowers know that I did not?

"You mean the verses about…" I muttered, reading out the words on the page I had turned to, knowing full well He knew all about my attempt to distract Him from what I had *really* been reading on the previous page – the words about "As the Father sent Him".

"No, Jill. The verses you just hurried by. 'As the Father has sent Me, I am sending you!'" He said much louder than before.

"I'm past that bit –"

"I'd noticed!"

Reluctantly, I turned back the page.

"Do you understand what it means?" He asked me again.

"Er, I think so. It means the Father sent You."

"Yes?"

"You came," I added more reluctantly than ever, "at Christmas." The fragrance from the roses was overpowering.

"I just had to come," He said simply. "Now, as the Father sent Me – I am sending you!"

"Like – in person?"

"That's how I came."

"Like 'Immanuel'?"

Silence. Then, "An 'Immanuel ministry' is a ministry of presence, Jill."

"Why didn't the Father send an angel?" I asked a little desperately. This conversation was not going in the direction I wanted it to.

"Angels are 'servants' of those He sends. They helped to strengthen Me when I came and it was hard."

And I remembered how angels had been near him in all those places – at Bethlehem, in Gethsemane, and at Calvary. I was disappointed. If He didn't send an angel instead of sending Jesus, the Father was not going to send an angel instead of sending me!

"Couldn't I send a letter or one of my books?" I enquired hopefully, returning to the matter at hand. "Or, or – I could send money. And they're collecting clothes to send at the church. (I needed to clear my cupboards out anyway!) Then, after more silence, rather petulantly, "It's so far to go. I'd have to get into one more plane and fly over one more ocean and you know I don't feel safe up there in the air – I like my feet on *terra firma*!"

"*Terra firma* is swinging around in space too!" He commented with a smile.

That didn't help.

"It's so far from home," I tried.

"Yes," He said. That was all, just "yes". What was that supposed to mean? Then suddenly I felt ashamed. How far had He come from His home in the High Countries to the Low Countries where I lived so He could "take me home" with Him one day?

"Maybe I could send an email," I began again, not willing to give up completely. "Or one of my video tapes? I have a good one called *Ministry According to Jesus*."

"It's better to have a ministry of presence," He said, interrupting my nonsense.

I knew He was right. And I also knew that the conversation had come to an end. So I left the Steps and walked back through the Christmas roses to the world He died for and started to pack. I needed to have a ministry of presence too. I knew there really was no other way.

When I got to Croatia with the ten women in my delegation, we had a briefing in Zagreb about the war. Afterwards one of the women asked, "What do we *do* when we get down to the border where the action is?"

"I've no idea," I replied.

"Well," asked another, "what do we *say* to these people, some of whom have seen their daughters raped and their husbands' throats cut and have lost everything?"

"I really don't know," I answered truthfully.

"Then why did you bring us?"

"To have a ministry of presence," I replied. And then, because they needed some help to get started, "If you want something to say, just say, 'We just had to come!'"

"That's all?" they asked doubtfully.

"Try it!" I said. And so on our way we went.

When we arrived everything was chaotic. At that point in the conflict about a thousand or so refugees were streaming over the border every day.

We set to, joining the aid workers in handing out food and clothing, and helping to process the women and children and the few men among them. (Refugee work is mainly with women and kids. The men are either fighting, in prison or dead)

On the second day, I arrived at the feeding station and looked around for my team. Each of them was in the middle of a group of women. Everybody had their arms around each other and there were lots of tears and hugging and noise!

I asked my interpreter to go around and see what my team was saying to the refugees as everyone was talking at once at the top of their voice and hanging onto each other for dear life. She came back puzzled. "Well, they are all saying the same thing," she said.

"And what's that?" I asked.

"They are all saying, 'I just had to come,' " she answered. I laughed out loud, and suddenly the fragrance was there again – Christmas roses!

"And what are the refugees saying to my women?" I asked the interpreter, who was looking a little bewildered.

"Well, they're all saying the same thing too," she responded. "They are all saying, 'You came! You came!'"

And then, in the middle of all the pain and confusion, the

noise and the weeping, I was back on the Steps of my soul in the Deep Place where nobody goes, thanking Him for sending me – in person – and letting me bring the team of women along so we could all have a ministry of presence together, just as He had done.

"You're welcome," He said. "It's for your sake as well as theirs!"

And then I understood the verse in the Golden Book in real terms. An "Immanuel ministry" is a ministry like Jesus had – and wants His followers to have, too. I heard his voice distinctly then as I climbed back to the shallow places where everyone lives. "As the Father has sent Me, so I am sending you."

"It's best not to argue, Lord, isn't it," I said silently. "You know best!"

Lord, here am I — send me. Not my sister

or my brother, my pastor, doctor,

missionary or social worker. Me!

As God was in Christ reconciling the

world to Himself so You are in me.

I know where to start — I'll respond to a

need and when I get there I'll know what

to say! I'll say, "I just had to come!"

and that's where I'll begin! May they be

glad we came — You and I. Walk out of

my life to bless these people, Lord.

Amen

Christmas

SURPRISE

Hay in His hair, stars in His eyes,
God came visiting. What a surprise!
Walking down stars from the throne to my heart,
High King of heaven, how precious Thou art.

Crowned with my sin and hanging in space,
I see you in agony, blood on your face.
Whipped for my good, nailed to my cross,
Dying in pieces, careless of loss.

Poetry in motion as You rose from Your grave,
Loving me heavenwards, eager to save,
Reaching my hurts with Gilead's balm,
Smiling me strength, leading me home.

Calling for faith when I just want to die,
Insisting on trust when I don't want to try;
Urging me on when I quit in despair,
Being my sunbeam when shadows are there.

Holding me still when I just want to run,
Smiling me strength, leading me home.
Reach into my soul and help it stand tall,
Give me the power to fulfil my call.

Power in motion that speaks of Your might,
Gives You the glory, gives You Your rights.
Even to grey hairs, visit my day;
Make me to You useful – spend me away.

Ignite my poor faith till it dances in praise,
Multiply grace for the rest of my days.
Send me, and spend me for ones who don't know,
You came here to visit such a long time ago.

Hay in Your hair, stars in Your eyes,
God in Christ present. What a surprise!

Surprise me all over again, dear Precious Friend:

Saving God, Present Saviour, and Powerful Spirit.

Reduce me to a proper size in my own eyes. Grow in me a

simple faith that leans hard, learns more of Your glory and fixes

its compass on the North Star – pointing me to Your house –

the one with the beautiful estate and the gorgeous garden with

English roses everywhere! Thank You for coming to visit.

Thank you that You decided to stay long enough

to invite me over to Your place – forever.

Amen

VICTORIA

━━━━━━━━ ∽◌∾ ━━━━━━━━

*T*WAS IN EUROPE AT CHRISTMAS. A luncheon had been arranged in a country club. Three men had paid for 200 women to have lunch and listen to a speaker: the speaker was me. As far as the three men could tell, most of the women were not believers in Christ. They had planned it that way. They just didn't tell me till I was at the door!

We had refreshments on the covered terrace. I looked around and felt decidedly nervous. Leaving the chatter in a myriad of European languages, though most spoke English, I went inside, took the Golden Book out and looked at the passage of Scripture I had planned to use. This was not the crowd I was prepared for.

He came and sat beside me.

"Oh, Lord, I'm so glad. I didn't know You'd been invited!"

"What are you going to tell them?" He asked.

"Well that's it – I don't know now. I thought they were all going to be church people. I'm so glad you've come, Lord, they're really intimidating – these 'ultra-suede ladies'. Look at their clothes…"

"Look at their hearts." He replied.

Then they all came into the dining room and there was no time to redo my notes or anything. Now I was really nervous! I put my head down as if I was looking for something under the table and prayed!

"I'm not under the table, Jill!" He teased me.

I had been so absorbed I hadn't seen her come in.

"I feel drawn to you. I think you can help me," she said softly. Then awkwardly, "I don't know what I mean really. I don't do this sort of thing!"

I looked up to find an English girl – young and very beautiful. She sat down by the table at my feet and waited expectantly.

I felt awkward having her there at my feet, but she appeared to be quite relaxed and the other guests didn't seem to think it strange. Perhaps her clothing gave her away. She was festooned with crystals and emblems that told me she was in to all sorts of New Age thought and philosophies, and probably quite used to sitting on the floor – to meditate!

"Tell me about yourself," I said. She looked a little startled – English women aren't used to being asked to talk about themselves. "What's your story?" I encouraged her. "Tell me about your spiritual journey."

"I've come to a place where I know there is something more," she said. "I've always had this sense of belonging somewhere else, wherever I am. You know – something I'm missing."

"There was a writer who really helped me when I felt like that," I said. "He was called C. S. Lewis. He wrote: 'If I find in myself a desire that no experience in this world can satisfy, the probable explanation is I was made for another world.'"★

Her eyes flickered with some sort of inner recognition.

"I think you may be searching for God," I said. "Do you have a religious philosophy?"

"Not *one*," she said, somewhat disapprovingly. "You can't have just *one*. Who is wise enough to say one is worth more than another?" She continued, warming to the conversation, "Oh, I've lots of beliefs, bits and pieces blended together, but not just one."

"Look at her heart," the Lord said again. "She's hungry, so hungry. I am the bread of life."

I knew that Victoria was typical of Europe's postmodern worshippers and searchers after truth who openly acknowledge the confusion inside, the heart hunger

★ From *Mere Christianity*

that won't quit and the lifestyle that won't satisfy. They have a yearning too deep for words and too insistent to be ignored.

"Until you find the one true God, you will always feel there's a hole in your heart," I told her. Then before she could say anything I asked her, "Which of all the philosophical and religious beliefs you hold has helped you the most? What is it that has led you towards one truth that has seemed to be more true than other truths?"

"Astrology," she answered without hesitation.

"You know," I said, "there were some incredibly brilliant astrologers who lived 2,000 years ago and who, at great cost to themselves, took a long journey one Christmas, to a manger in a town called Bethlehem. They knelt down and worshipped a baby boy they found, lying in a cattle stall in a bale of hay."

I looked at Victoria and said, "Victoria, you have to decide who that baby is. They believed He was God – the God of all gods in heaven and on earth. They acknowledged Him as the Lord of their lives. Their astrology led them to that baby. That baby grew up and led them to heaven."

It was a miracle that the people stayed at their tables in the dining room and we were left alone to talk. I had all the time I needed to say what I wanted about Christmas to a girl that God had taken me halfway around the world to meet. I looked at her, loved her and said, "You have to meet Him at the manger! You have to figure out who the baby is."

"Do you think there's hope for me?" she asked me quietly.

"Oh yes!" I said. "I believe you are going to find what you have been looking for all your life. But Victoria, the Word of God says, 'You will find Him if you search for Him with all your heart.' You have to make this a priority." I knew she would.

All of us have to meet Him at the manger. We have to decide who this baby is. Is He just the founder of one more religion in the world? Or just another Jewish child, born in extraordinary times in an extraordinary place in an extraordinary way? Or is He the North for the compass of our searching hearts? Some of us have to bring our long-held religious beliefs to kneel at the manger, just like the astrologers (or kings) brought theirs so long ago. If it is true that "God was in Christ reconciling the world to Himself," then all other religions have to meet Him at the manger, kneel down and submit to Christ.

"O dear Lord," I asked Him, "Show her who You are!"

I believe I heard Him say, "I will."

KNEELING WITH KINGS

Kneeling with kings at the crib of my Saviour,
Singing in praise with the angels on high;
Here with Your people, wondering about You,
I'm thinking of Jesus and wanting to cry!

Father, I love You for giving me heaven
Wrapped in the form of a newborn so small,
But how could You stand to know all that would happen
When You left Him in Beth'lem in an animal stall?

Treasured in glory and praised by creation
God as a baby to humans on loan:
Why didn't You run down the stairway of heaven,
Snatch up Your God Child and take Him back home?

What's that You're saying? You left Him to save me?
You love me as much as You love your sweet Son?
You gave me Your heart when You gave me Your Jesus
And my Father's full giving is only begun.

I bring You my life and the years lent for living
For Your crib-and-cross sacrifice tear me apart:
When You count all my tears as I kneel at this altar
May You know it worthwhile when You look at my heart!

THE GARDEN OF GRACE

THE GARDEN OF GRACE

COMFORT

SOMEBODY'S
PRAYING FOR ME

"...HE ALWAYS LIVES TO INTERCEDE FOR THEM."
Hebrews 7:25

IT WAS A DARK DAY. I was running on empty and I didn't want to get up. I had to of course. There was work to be done; people to see. As I dressed, my spirits began to lift. They lifted and lifted and lifted! I was alone in the house, and by now I was preparing a breakfast I had earlier thought I couldn't eat because of the knot in my stomach. I stood still in the kitchen. By this time my heart wanted to tap dance!

Wonderingly, I asked myself, What's happening? And then, with sudden understanding, I thought of all my friends who knew about my dark day and had promised to intercede.

"Oh," I said out loud. "That's what's happening, *somebody's praying for me!*" And then it came – a voice as clear as a bell said, "I Am!" I was immobile, savouring the moment! Of course, He ever lives to intercede for us! Of course, of course, of course! I opened the door of the day and went out!

Lord Jesus Christ, thank You for being
my heavenly intercessor!
Thank You for ever-living and praying for
me. When I'm running out of prayers, help
me to share my dark days with my friends.
And remind me often that You are the great
I Am who ever lives to pray for me.

Amen

WHO PUT OUT THE STARS?

"HE IS THE LIGHT OF THE WORLD."
John 8:12

AVE THE STARS EVER GONE out in your life? Is it dark? Too dark to read the Golden Book and find some light to comfort your heart? I understand.

Who put out the stars? What child rebelled? Who left home? Who came back a stranger? Who hates you so? He that loved you so? What happened? Who put out the stars in your eyes? Did it happen when a dream died?

I had a dream that died. I dreamed that my mother would come to see us when we emigrated to America. That she would come and see where we had made our home and meet our church people and receive their love. I so wanted to see her just walk into the door of the sanctuary, I would stand in the lobby of the church on a Sunday morning and imagine that the ladies with the grey hair were my mum! Sometimes one, bent and worn, would come through the doors and tears would spring to my eyes and I would catch my breath. If only…

I wanted her to come so badly it made me sick at heart. I wanted the children to take her out to the pumpkin farm at Thanksgiving and for her to walk in the shopping mall with us. I wanted her to go to a baseball game. I wanted her in my home, in my life, in Christ, in my arms. I wanted her in my new country for which we had left two newly widowed mothers, a lifetime of friends and our England. I had a dream, and while I had my dream the stars shone.

The years went by and sometimes the dream nearly happened to come true. But after many years my dream died – because she died and she never came. She never came to understand why we had left England for Jesus' sake. And she never really knew how much my hungry heart grieved to leave her behind.

It was after that day when the stars went out that He met me

Comfort

on the Steps of my soul; He lit a candle for me in the darkness and helped me bury my dream by its light. And He put up a marker. I could hardly read it by the light of the candle but I managed to make out the words, "Now she understands!" And then the lights went on! The stars came out again. And I went on my way, willing to wait till the day He who is the brightest and most shiny Day Star of all will light up all of heaven for my sweet mother and me!

What put the stars out in your life? When someone puts the stars out in your life run to the Steps of your soul (be careful you don't trip in the dark). Go Heart Deep and find Him waiting there. He will light a candle for you so you can see to read the Golden Book together. You'll find strength to bury the dead dream and not keep the corpse for company! Once that's done you can blow out the candle – and then He'll switch on the starlight again, not only in the sky but in your eyes! And you'll say, "All's well with the world!" And it will be.

This is how it happened with me. The Steps were wet with dew when I arrived. I sat on them anyway. I shivered. It was so dark; not a glimmer of light.

The stars were usually so brilliant when I watched them from there, I swear it seemed that the Steps were only a mile away from God's galaxy of Grace. I usually felt I could reach out and touch the beautiful things. So many stars! But on this night I couldn't see one of them!

The Golden Book lay by me, but there was no way I could read it of course.

"Who put the stars out in your life, Jill?" I jumped. I hadn't seen Him come in the darkness. Silence. Then His dear voice came again.

"Who put out the stars?" He knew and I knew He knew. I knew He knew I knew!

I thought about His question about the black sadness in my heart. And I knew He wanted me to say the words we both knew out loud.

"A dream died," I said.

"Ahh."

You don't always have to say things out loud when you are sitting on the Steps of your soul in the darkness, but it helps sometimes. It helps because it's said. It's out there to be addressed.

"Any death is hard," He said seriously. "Especially the death of a mother. Death is the antithesis of everything I had in mind. It is not what I dreamed for the human race. I thought long and hard about that.

"You had a dream that died?" I murmured. Then I thought about Eden and how the darkness came and the stars went out. And I thought about the cross – the most dreadful day in the world when He hung between the earth and the heavens, and darkness covered us all and… and… "The stars went out," I said.

"Yes."

"Who put out the stars in your sky, Jill?" He asked again.

"You know what happened, Lord."

"When someone puts out the stars," He said, "I will light a candle for you so we can see the Golden Book and you can find some comfort there." And suddenly, there it was – a candle in His hands and a soft sweet light springing into the shadows of death. He opened the Book at special places that were just right. And He read me the stories of real people whose dreams had died. There's lots about that in the Golden Book: David's dream for his favourite son, Absalom; and Hagar for her son, Ishmael. I noticed most of the dreams that died had to do with Heart Deep relationships.

The light was soft and warm and the shadows couldn't stay once He had lit the candle. Afterwards, He closed the Golden Book and took my hand and helped me to bury my dream by the light of the candle He was holding for me.

When it was over He gently blew out the candle. When I saw Him do that I protested, "No Lord, I don't want the darkness to swallow me up again." But He just smiled and did it anyway.

Amazing grace! "Let there be light," He said and there was! As I looked up wonderingly – Stars! They were back!

Star light, star bright: light my life.
Daystar from on high
Do not pass me by;
See me shiver in the night: light my light.
Amen

CLEAR AIR

ℋOW WAS IT THAT EACH TIME I went to the Deep Place where nobody goes, far from the shallow place where everyone lives, I began to breathe more easily? I noticed it one day as I sat on the Steps of my soul and waited for the springtime.

Actually it's always springtime there outside the Front Door. It's only me that brings the winter with me to the Meeting Place. It takes a little while to feel the springtime in my heart, but as the Spirit's quiet warmth begins to do the melting, I take a deep breath and notice – clear air, so clear!

Waiting for Him to come, I played with words about it:

Clear air,
No pollution here.
Spirit of the living God breathe over me

Son-warmed breeze of blessings blow,
No frosty faith can stay so frozen here
that Son-shine and the breeze of God

cannot but breathe these embers red –
And fire appear.

Life light,
No dreaded twilight zone can dim.
God's glory blaze –
Illuminate my way,
Chase shadows far, lift up my head to light my path of
        service clear.
May I see footprints – easy to follow after.

Spirit of the Living One,
Fill all the parts in me – till God is all in all
And I stand tall and straight, marching as to war!

Soft touch of angel wings
Remind me of Thy loving rule
O Spirit, "gentle me", I who am so rough and rude,
Cared for and watched over till the day –
Home safe, I breathe in clear air – warm breath of God.
        Oh joy!

Devotion

A STILLING OF THE SOUL

"THEY THAT WAIT UPON THE LORD
WILL RENEW THEIR STRENGTH…"
Isaiah 40:31

———— ❧ ————

"HOW WILL THAT STRENGTH come to me, Lord?"

"By a 'stilling of the soul' in My Presence."

"A calm?"

"Maybe."

"A sense of 'Everything is all right' when I know everything is still all wrong? Isn't this denial?"

"No, it's faith. You live in the 'It will be all right' instead of the 'This will never end.'"

"O Lord, the problem is my soul dashes about inside me, frantic with having to stop doing all the things that must be done."

"Tell it to sit down and listen to Me. There must first be a stilling of the soul."

And so I took my soul to task and brought my will to bear on the matter. And I "waited".

Sitting in the silence
Of this waiting room with You,
I'm ready and I'm willing
For You to tell me what to do.
I revel in Your presence,
Hear the whispers of your grace,
Shattered by the love light
In your eyes and on your face.

So hush my heart to listen,
Quit your pacing, now be still.
Ready all your senses
To discern His perfect will.
Learning His directives
In the Spirit's clear air,
Thankful in the stillness
For this priceless gift of prayer

Lord, I wait — till there is a stilling of the soul within me.

Then, and then only, will I speak. Amen

Devotion

THE "YES" OF THE SOUL

I AM LEARNING THAT WHEN God asks me to do a hard thing, a lonely thing, an only thing, He requires an answer. The sooner I can give it, the better for my soul! I need to yield to God's words from the Golden Book to me. But what is yielding? I've come to call it the "Yes" of my soul.

The "yes" of the soul is my language of love
As I yield up my life to the Father above,
Asking for help to obey His direction,
Seeking for heart grace in deep soul reflection,
Needing to grasp His good purpose and will,
Knowing I need to be quiet and still.

The Lord mists the meadows of this garden of grace
And we walk and we talk in this marvellous place.
His rainbows of promise shaft all through my sky
And that gets me to wonder why I always ask "Why
All the sorrow and grief are allowed to remain?"
And the dark clouds oppress me and the deep-seated pain
Never quits, so it seems, as I sink in despair
Yet it's worth it, dear Jesus, to see You standing there!

Then I dare lift my head and praise You anew
For the dark things, the hard things, that You lead me
     through.
Hear the "yes" of my soul, it's my language of love
As I yield all I am to the Father above.
I'll trust You for power for the life that You've planned,
Till I'm home safe and sound in Immanuel's land!

Devotion

WHAT WOULD DADDY DO?

⸺ ⸺ ⸺ ☙ ⸺ ⸺ ⸺

HAVE YOU EVER BEEN CONFUSED about a decision that has to be made? Maybe you don't know whether to continue a relationship or take another job opportunity. It could be that you are wondering about your elderly parents and how best to care for them? How do you know what God wants you to do? It's not always clear is it?

A long time ago I needed to make a difficult choice over a matter and tried to sort it out myself. Not that I didn't pray a lot about it, but I couldn't seem to hear what God was saying to me. Even though I read the Golden Book, diligently searching for clues, and spent much time in secret with Jesus alone, it seemed murky at best! The only thing I began to see was the better I knew the Lord, the better I would see clearly the way to go.

In the middle of this dilemma my father died, leaving my sister and her husband running the family motor car business. I was on the board of directors and had to travel back to the UK for the funeral. While I was home we had a board meeting for the family business.

My father had left things in good shape for my sister and her husband, and the board had known my dad forever, or so it seemed, so there was a great spirit of harmony around the table. Then someone raised a question that caused a problem.

I had no idea what was going on as I was only a "sleeping partner", so I just sat quietly and listened. (I also know little about finances and to this day I am tempted to open another account when my cheque book gets in a mess!)

The conversation came to a stop. Nobody knew the answer to the problem. And as the people round the table began to argue the different sides of the issue, it seemed impossible to see a way forward.

There was silence for a moment and then my sister, who had been my father's business partner, said musingly, almost to herself, "What would Daddy do?"

There was silence as everyone went to work on that. Then light dawned almost simultaneously round the table as person after person spoke about what my father would have done if he were alive. The answer became clearer all the time. All the board members had known my father well, although not as well as my sister, who was confidently bringing a consensus and making decisions that ended up being unanimous!

I couldn't wait for some peace and quiet back at my sister's house. I knew everyone would be out and about busying themselves with things that had to be done in the aftermath of a funeral. When all was quiet I went to my room and ran to the Deep Place.

"Lord."

"How are things going?" He asked.

"You know, Lord!"

"Yes, but it helps you to tell me anyway. So tell me how the board meeting went!"

"You know, Lord," I began excitedly. "You know about my dilemma once I get back to the States. Well, when my sister said 'What would Daddy do?' it suddenly threw light on my questions and how to get an answer. I thought to myself, What would You do, Lord? What would my Heavenly Father want done? And then I knew!"

"The better you know Me, the better you will know what to do," He said. It was both simple and profound. Some words from an old hymn popped into my head,

Take time to be holy, speak oft with thy Lord;
Abide in Him always, and feed on His Word…

Then again…

Take time to be holy, let Him be thy guide;
And run not before Him, whatever betide;
In joy or in sorrow still follow thy Lord,
And, looking to Jesus, still trust in His Word.

W.D Longstaff

Yes, yes ! As I take time to get to know my Father God, the light of His Spirit will bring sweet understanding in the darkest tunnels I traverse. I left the UK feeling a distinct impression in my spirit of which way to set about sorting out the mess I faced back home.

Do you know the right thing to do in your dilemmas? How to behave, react, speak or stay silent? Ask yourself, "What would Daddy do?" Get to know your loving Heavenly Father, day by day. The better you know Him, the clearer His will and way will be.

Father, teach me to know You so well that I will know

what to do when it's time to take a stand,

make some hard choice, or plan what I'm planning!

Abba Father, I love You.

Your grateful redeemed one, Jill

SO LITTLE REDEEMED

Over recent years, I have collected old, devotional Christian classics. The one I was reading on this particular day – *The Prayer that Spans the World* – was a wonderful book on the Lord's Prayer written by Helmut Thielicke, a Lutheran pastor and theologian in mid-twentieth-century Germany. In it he mentions being "so little redeemed".

The phrase riveted my attention. I wanted to talk to Jesus about it so I went to Him early, before the day began. "Early" is precious time. But the older I get, the harder "early" becomes! Unfortunately, I had written in a book about prayer that "Sleep deprivation is better than God deprivation", so now I had to follow my own advice; I had to do without a little sleep to go to the Deep Place where nobody goes, before the Shallow Place where everyone lives got moving at the light of day. I was so glad I went!

"I have been reading an old book, Lord."

"When you read a new book, it's a good idea to read an old one!" He said.

We were sitting on the Steps of my soul by this time and I was excited. I knew we would have a wonderful time reading from the greatest book of all – the classic of classics – the Golden Book. He had been underlining Scriptures that talked about redemption for me with a Majesty marker. After I had read these verses I murmured, "Thank you for redeeming me."

He didn't answer at once but pointed out a passage in Thielicke's book; the very one that had caught my eye. *The Prayer that Spans the World* is a record of a series of sermons he had preached against a background of falling bombs towards the end of the Second World War. By the seventh sermon only the choir loft of his beautiful church in Stuttgart was left standing. But he didn't give up. (That's what makes this book so incredible.)

It made riveting reading. He talks of the human race being like a child lost in a forest calling out, "Father, are you there?" Then Thielicke writes, "God is always there. And you can call Him Father." His wartime congregation, suffering and dying, must have hoped fervently that he was right about the Father part.

There was also a man in Germany called Nietzsche whose writings and philosophy were a great influence on both Hitler and Stalin. One day Thielicke went to talk to him about Christ redeeming the world.

Nietzsche responded, "You Christians will have to look a lot more redeemed for me, Nietzsche, to believe in your redeemer!"

"What a devastating thing Nietzsche said," I commented.

"Yes!"

"I wonder if he would have listened to Thielicke if his experience with Christians who, apparently, had not practised what they preached had been any different?" I mused.

Then He and I talked about the cross and what it cost Him to die in my place. Overwhelmed, I was on my knees again, asking Him to forgive me for being one of those "so little redeemed" people.

"How dare I be so little redeemed, Lord?"

He didn't answer and I cried then, not for me (which is usually why I cry) but for Jesus and what my sin caused Him to suffer. Then He left me and for the first time that morning I looked at my watch. It was about time for the world to get up, but before I left to do my work I wrote Him a note and posted it through the prayer mail box. It said:

So little redeemed,
So little like Him,
So little I've changed from what I have been.
So little like Jesus so people can see
His power and His glory
Living in me.

So little redeemed,
So my friends cannot see
The Risen Lord Jesus
Living in me.
Why then should they listen
When I tell them of Him?
When I'm so little changed
From what I have been?

So little redeemed
I'm ashamed of myself,
I want transformation
And spiritual wealth.
So I'm going to surrender,
So that people can see
The living Lord Jesus
Living in me!

If I understand what redemption means I will realize I am not my own, I am bought with a price – the blood of Christ!

Lord, are there those who would say I have

stopped them from considering the gospel

because I am "so little redeemed"? Forgive me.

Remind me I am watched by others!

Amen

Devotion

COME EARLY

"VERY EARLY IN THE MORNING, WHILE IT WAS STILL DARK
JESUS GOT UP, LEFT THE HOUSE AND WENT OFF TO A
SOLITARY PLACE, WHERE HE PRAYED."
Mark 1:35

I HAD AWOKEN SUDDENLY ONE MORNING. Why I don't know; it was long before light dawned. So I had reached for the Golden Book to read a little and turned to words about the Lord healing Peter's wife's mother. I was struck by the verse that followed shortly after this event and wondered what He had wanted to talk to God about so early that day?

"COME EARLY," a voice said in my ear! Then I knew that He wanted me to get up too!

Once I was sitting on the Steps of my soul and He was beside me – we had a lovely talk about it.

"I read in your book, Lord Jesus, about the morning You healed Peter's wife's mother, and how that evening the whole town gathered at the door!"

"It was a busy night!"

"The trauma in the morning and then all those folk healed.

All those demons thrown out of people – You must have been exhausted."

"Tired, but happy."

I wondered how He had woken up without an alarm clock. Maybe He asked one of His beautiful cockerels to crow outside His window before dawn!

"I knew the news of the healings would spread and the crowds would return soon," He was saying, "and I needed to talk to My Father."

"And then your four new recruits came after You, excited about the campaign getting off to such a great start, and found You! 'Everyone's looking for You,' they said. And then You said, 'Let's go somewhere else!' What on earth did they say to that?"

"I told them I needed to keep My focus and go to the small villages and towns that hadn't heard the good news of God. That was why I had come."

"Was that what You wanted to talk to Your Father about? Whether You should ride the wave of Your popularity and take advantage of the miracles?"

He didn't answer, but somehow I knew.

In the silence the conviction came to me that – in my little way – I must not let the crowds determine my ministry either, only God. Then I got out of bed, made myself a cup of coffee, and took my invitations from a file and laid them out before the Lord.

Suddenly I was afraid. What would happen if I made wrong

choices, allowed others to use me or direct me for their own ends or ministries? Or what if I was flattered by a *big* opportunity and missed the right one? How would I know what to do and where to go?

"COME EARLY," He said. "Then you'll know!" And my words came easily.

> "Cradle me, Lord."
> *"Underneath and all around are the everlasting arms."*
> "Steady me, Lord."
> *"I am a Rock, stand firm!"*
> "Give me wisdom beyond myself."
> *"I am your wisdom."*
> "Show me the way."
> *"I Am the way!"*
> "Drench me with the gentle dew of heaven. Freshen my faith."
> *"COME EARLY then – before the wheels of life start turning."*
> "Here I am!"
> *"I know!"*

JOY!

TILL I GET HOME ONE EASTER

"VERY EARLY ON THE FIRST DAY OF THE WEEK,
JUST AFTER SUNRISE, THEY WERE ON THE WAY TO THE
TOMB AND THEY ASKED EACH OTHER, 'WHO WILL ROLL
THE STONE AWAY FROM THE ENTRANCE OF THE TOMB?'
BUT WHEN THEY LOOKED UP, THEY SAW THAT THE STONE,
WHICH WAS VERY LARGE, HAD BEEN ROLLED AWAY."
Mark 16:2–4

T WAS EARLY AT THE FRONT DOOR. The Steps of my soul were wet with the dew of heaven. I opened the Golden Book and turned to the resurrection story. It was Easter Sunday.

It was hard to read as I had come with a hurt that wouldn't allow me to "hear" any of His promises and was therefore making me physically sick! A situation in the family had broken my heart. "I need to concentrate," I told myself severely.

I read about the angels rolling away the stone. Here were the women, bravely going to the tomb where Jesus had been laid after the crucifixion. They knew there was a huge stone across the doorway. "Who shall roll away the stone?" they asked. "Who will roll away the stone?" When they got there it was rolled away!

All that worry for nothing! I thought.

Suddenly He came. I worshipped Him, thanking Him with all my heart for Easter! Even the birds joined in the praise.

"Lord, these women are so like me!" I said, showing Him the passage I was reading. (It really helps to read the Golden Book with Him and get His insights on it. After all He was there!)

"I spend my life worrying about piles of problems up ahead that seem far too big for my small strength, Lord. Obstacles that tower over my thoughts all day long."

"But you know, Jill, that if you trust Me to be ahead of you, and go on with your life and service for Me, that usually when you get to the dreaded problem the stone has been rolled away! Walk in faith towards the tomb of your troubles," He advised. "Believe that if God can raise the dead, He can bring life into this situation too, whatever the circumstances."

So we sat and talked about the incredible words in the Golden Book about the stone being rolled away and the tomb being empty when the women came.

"What was it like when the angels rolled the stone away and let You out, Lord?" I asked. Then He was laughing and it sounded as if the whole of creation was laughing too. Great glad cries of "He is risen! He is risen!"

"The angels didn't let me out, Jill," He said gently. "I was

long gone, bursting the shackles of death, out into the light of all that's living. The angels didn't open the tomb to let Me out, but to let the women in!"

Then I was part of the laughter of praise that wouldn't quit all around me. For these moments I had forgotten my pain, born out of a precious child close to me who was suffering greatly. My heart had been red raw and my spirit crushed when I came to the Steps, and I had had a few minutes blessed respite. Suddenly, the situation intruded into my mind again and it was like a tsunami swamping everything in and around me.

I gasped for breath and cast a desperate look at Him sitting on the Steps outside the Front Door. Why had I never noticed a boulder at the side of the door lintel?

"It's the Stone," He said. "I put it there to remind you of the power of My resurrection life."

I don't know how long we read the Golden Book together that Easter morning, but I know it was a turning point for me. I had to say a prayer in our church services that day and the words came easily as a response to my own time with my Lord and Saviour Jesus Christ in the Deep Place where nobody goes.

This is the prayer. I want to pray it with you as I prayed it for the congregation and I would like to think you will step inside my words and make it your own.

Turn my crying and my sighing
Into laughter in the rain,
Bend to bless my raw emotions
Lying prostrate in their pain.
Help me leave the graveside singing,
Trust myself to Your great might.
O dear Lord, refresh my spirit,
Pierce my darkness with Your light.

Walk into my deadness shouting,
"I'm alive, lift up your eyes,
For the tomb of all your troubles

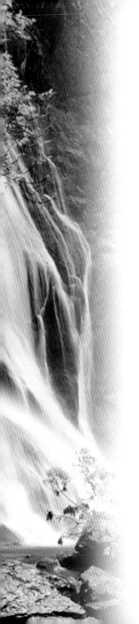

By my life can be surprised."
He who raised His Christ at Easter
Has the power to impart
All the Spirit's grand dynamic
To my fainting, failing heart.

You can do it if I let You
You're the best that life can be,
This the reason for Golgotha
For Your dying agony.
Where to find the healing medicine
That reaches deep inside?
It is in Your resurrection,
It's the reason that You died.

On Good Friday You took all my sins
And paid for all my mess,
So it must be galling now to see
My life so passionless.
Forgive my cool indifference
To Your searing sufferings,
My meagre grudging service,
My small change in offerings!

O Jesus, mercy on me
When the souls for whom You died

Easter

Don't know it broke Your Father's heart
When You were crucified.
My flimsy faith must grieve You
My trivial life depress
The One who gave His child away
To win me 'Ever-ness.'

In the heat of all my heartaches
Send the Spirit's cooling balm,
In this magic melting moment
Cradle me within Your arms.
Send Your Pentecostal Spirit
Drench me with Your saving Grace,
God forgive my part in causing
All those tears on Your face.

In this hallowed Easter moment
May I find new hope in Thee,
By Your fragrant precious presence
O dear Lord, lay hold of me.
Till I get home one Easter
And I hear the angels sing,
And You mend my broken image
And You heal my everything.

Then the crooked will be straightened
And the blind shall see Your Throne,
The orphans find a Father
And the homeless find a home.
The rejected have a family
And the twisted mind be sane,
Then the tortured won't remember
All the horror and the pain.

There the poor will have a mansion,
And the rich one share his wealth,
The refugee a country
And the little child her health.
When our strong, eternal bodies
Run besides eternal streams,
Then the miracle of heaven
Will exceed our wildest dreams.

So take my numbered moments
That You've counted out for me,
And help me live them as You did
In light of Calvary.
And when I get home one Easter
And I see You in that hour,
May I bring my lost world with me
By Your resurrection power!

Easter

YOU WORE MY THORNS

You wore my thorns, that I may know Your grace,
Pierced by my sin, that I may see Your face
There you forgave my sin and deep disgrace.
You wore my thorns, You wore my thorns.

You wore my robe, You let them mock and sneer,
You took the beating You knew I could not bear,
In this silent moment, I turn and see You there.
You wore my robe, You wore my robe.

You felt my nails and watched the hammer fall,
Legions of angels You refused to call,
Watched they who loved You, grieving and appalled
You felt my nails, You felt my nails.

You bore my cross, You bore Your father's frown,
Tears on His face, His judgment took You down.
Now it's my turn to wear the thorny crown
For You bore my cross, You bore my cross.

You died my death, You gave Your life for me
Laid in my tomb of sin, You set me free
You loved a girl, who hurt You terribly
You died my death, You died my death.

Teach me to love what once I so despised,
Live for Your smile, the love-light in Your eyes,
Ignite a flame of love that never dies,
You wore my thorns, You wore my thorns!

Easter

FATHER DEEP

My EPIPHANY OF JESUS occurred at college in the UK. I was a child of a world war – the Second World War, in case you are wondering!

I can't remember often sleeping in my little pink and white bedroom; mostly in an air raid shelter. I lived in Liverpool, which was not a good place to be as we were bombed every night! One night when the blitz seemed never-ending, I frantically recited the Apostles' Creed I had learned at school prayers.

"I believe in God *the Father Almighty* Maker of heaven and earth," I whispered desperately. This was the first time I can remember being "Heart Deep" in my wonderings about the "Father-ness" of God. To a small child waiting to be buried by a bomb in an air raid shelter the world seemed mightily *un*Fatherly to me! Yet the Father *was* there in the dark forest of my fears. I began to hear His voice, yes I did, and I found myself asking, "Father, is that You?"

I had no way of knowing, of course, that at about that time the great German theologian Helmut Thielicke was preaching a sermon about the Fatherness of God in the ruins of his church building in Stuttgart to what was left of his congregation. The city was staggering under the last paroxysm of the war. He talked about the lost-ness of mankind being like the tragedy of a child who had lost his Father. The inner situation of the heart of man was described by him as follows: "Man is walking through the dark forest of life in the gloom of night. Spectres are looming all around and strange noises disquiet him. The dark forest is full of dangers."

Thielicke continued: "Everything will be all right so long as we hear His good voice calling to us above the howling of the wolves, above the sound of branches snapping, above the ominous noises around us, God is always there." Those few listeners must have wondered mightily how this could be.

Meanwhile, hundreds of miles away across the English Channel, I clutched my mother, my sister and my gas mask in the dark shelter, and tried to listen for His voice "in the forest" above the sirens and the horrible din of war. "Father, is that You?" my small heart cried. "Is that you?" And I wondered *if* perchance it

THE GARDEN OF GRACE

was indeed the Father, He could bring me out of the forest of my Fatherless life.

I took my spiritual confusion with me to college. Like most post-war British students, I was struggling with eternal questions such as what sort of an Almighty God was in heaven (if indeed heaven "was"): *Is He there? Does He care? Is He fair?* What was more, I felt a strange obligation to make use of the reprieve I had been given by surviving the Liverpool blitz. I had a vague sense of needing to use my life for some meaningful purpose.

A dramatic stay in Addenbrookes Hospital, and an encounter with a nurse who led me thoroughly and irrevocably to Christ and His cause was the culmination of my epiphany.

Living Heart Deep is living *in* the Fatherness of God. Held hard against His heart you can let the wolves howl, the shadows deepen, the branches snap and the wind whine (all Thielicke's images), but you can walk through the forest with your head held high – God is always there!

Quotes from *The Prayer that Spans the World.*

HIS FATHER'S EYES

"ONE DAY JESUS WAS PRAYING IN A CERTAIN PLACE.
WHEN HE HAD FINISHED ONE OF HIS DISCIPLES SAID TO HIM,
'LORD TEACH US TO PRAY, JUST AS JOHN TAUGHT HIS DISCIPLES.'
HE SAID TO THEM, 'WHEN YOU PRAY SAY, FATHER.'"
Luke 11:1–2a

*T*WAS ON A PLANE (what's new?). I had been speaking on
the subject of a Fatherless race needing a Father and where to
find one. I was sitting by a middle-aged lady who asked me what
I was writing; so I told her I was writing about prayer.

"Do you pray?" I asked her."

"Of course, everybody prays," she answered.

"Who do you pray to?"

"God, I suppose."

"Which God would that be?"

"Well now, prayer is a lot more than praying to God you
know. I go within myself to meditate – calm myself down. In fact,
praying for me is creating peace for myself in the middle of all
the noise and confusion around me."

"Sounds sort of lonely!"

"What do you mean?"

"Just you and you!"

"I only want me," she replied somewhat defensively. "I'm enough. People have helped me – I used to have a low self-image. Prayer is where you're happy alone with yourself, where you sort of commune with yourself."

"So it's nothing to do with God your Father?"

"Not really. Sometimes, I suppose. But it doesn't have to be!"

Right where I was on that aeroplane, I flew to the Steps of my soul. "O Father, help me explain," I pleaded.

The conversation reminded me of a quote on the subject of prayer from a well known periodical published all the way back in the 1940s – just before the Second World War -– before TV, mobile phones, computers or Star Wars movies. I had it in my notes in the talk I had just given! I shared it with the lady.

People must engage in something like PRAYER and for the following reasons. People today are being constantly assaulted from the outside by so many things, like work, haste, telephones, correspondence, the hooting and clanging of traffic, the radio and movies that they absolutely must erect a wall to protect themselves against the avalanche of impressions and demands.

The best way to prevent one being completely absorbed and devoured by these impressions and claims is to enter into a state of inner composure which must offer a counterbalance to our present way of life which is constantly turned outward. This state of inner composure is undoubtedly similar to what the Christian calls prayer.

Naturally, when one engages in this inner soliloquy one need not act as if one were really speaking to a "Thou" to "God" one must be quite rational about it and abandon this old resort to a world beyond where one's most secret thoughts are supposedly heard. One must quite soberly make up one's mind that this is only a matter of talking to oneself for the purpose of clarifying and composing our minds.

Quoted in *The Prayer that Spans the World*

Helmut Thielicke went on to comment: "What a tragic delusion, this yearning for prayer which denies itself any actual fulfilment. Beyond the heroic, set face of this man lies the whole tragedy of a child who has lost his Father."

I looked at this lady sitting beside me seventy years later – she was Fatherless, too. But I had the secret! I knew she could go from Fatherless to Father-ness! I had to let her know. I rushed back to the Steps of my soul.

"Help me, Father, help me. Help me to tell her you came in Christ to this Fatherless world to fill her Fatherless heart. Help me explain," I asked urgently.

My mind went to the Gospel in the Golden Book. (That's what happens on the Steps of your soul, you remember all sorts of things you think you have forgotten!) and the place where it

told of Jesus in the upper room with Philip, who was demanding, "Show us the Father and it is enough." And the Lord replied, "He that has seen me has seen the Father!" In other words He said, "Look at *me*, Philip!"

Fatherness

Then I remembered another conversation I had had with the Lord about this. I had commented, "When he looked at You, Lord Jesus, Philip must have wondered why he had never noticed the family resemblance before: Did he see You had Your Father's eyes?"

I came back to the shallow place where everyone lives (and flies through the Father's heavens in metal tubes with wings) and found the lady still there waiting. Where else could she go? And I told her the old, old story of Jesus and His love.

We parted as new friends, and I pray for her and all the other people I meet on a daily basis that feel they live in a Father-*less* world and don't know about Father-*ness*.

Do you know anyone like that? Why not spend time Heart Deep talking to the Father about them?

THE GARDEN OF GRACE

THE BEAT OF
MY FATHER'S HEART

⎯⎯⎯⎯⎯⎯⎯ ⁓⦿⦿⁓ ⎯⎯⎯⎯⎯⎯⎯

I WELL REMEMBER SITTING by a roaring fire on a Sunday during the war years. Our family had fled the bombs that rained down on us one night, chasing us hundreds of miles away to the beautiful English Lake District.

The rain slashed against the pane like giant tears, and the thunder grumbled away as if it was angry it had to hang around all day. I didn't like storms much. After all I was only young – barely six years of age. I was old enough, however, to understand there was a battle going on involving everyone in the whole world. But at that moment the war all seemed very far away.

The fire was warm. My father was sitting in his big chair, relaxed and reading the paper. Besides I could see His face and that gave me some comfort! Suddenly, as if he was aware I needed a little bit of reassurance, he put down his paper and smiled at me.

"Come here, little girl," he said, in his soft, quiet but commanding voice. Then I was safe in his arms, lying against his shoulder and feeling the beat of his heart. Now, whatever the weather, I can watch the rain and listen to the thunder all day, I thought. *This is a grand place to be!* Why, my father is bigger than any old storm that beats against my window!

I have thought about that incident many times since. As the storms of sorrow swamped me at my mother's funeral, or I found myself alone and in danger as I have travelled the world, I have sought the reassurance of my Heavenly Father's presence. When the winds of worry whipped my confidence away as I faced gangs of wild young people during street evangelism, or joined Christians in hiding in restricted countries, I have glanced up to see my Father's face.

As floods of fear have risen in my spirit when I have waited in a hospital for results of frightening medical tests, I've heard my Heavenly Father say, "Come here, little girl." And I've climbed into His arms, leaned my head against His shoulder and murmured, "This is a grand place to be!"

As I rest in that safe place, believing my Father is bigger than any old storm that beats against the windows of my life, I can watch the rain and listen to the thunder and know it's all right. *For here I can hear the beat of my Father's heart!*

Do you need to hear the beat of your Father's heart just now? Climb into His arms – just where you are. He's waiting.

Can you hear the beat of His heart?

Fatherness

FRIENDS WITH JESUS' FRIENDS

"'YOU ARE MY FRIENDS IF YOU DO WHAT I COMMAND.'"
John 15:14

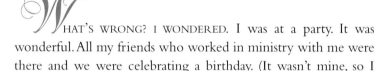

WHAT'S WRONG? I WONDERED. I was at a party. It was wonderful. All my friends who worked in ministry with me were there and we were celebrating a birthday. (It wasn't mine, so I could enjoy it!)

Somehow I didn't feel I was at the right party. Something was wrong. But I put the uneasiness out of my mind and joined in the fun. Afterwards we had a great time of prayer together and went our ways.

When I got in the car I noticed I wasn't alone! Oops, I'd better watch my speed!

"Lord, thank You for all my wonderful friends," I began. "I love it when we talk about You and read the Golden Book together. And when we sing and sing and it's so wonderful." And I began to realize how rich I was – with so very many Christian friends around and about filling my days with wholesome things to do.

Then I realized "we" – He and I – hadn't had a really long talk for ages.

"I'm sorry I haven't seen You in a while," I began, feeling a stab of guilt. "Lord, it's just that I've been so busy with ministry and – friends and things."

"Jill, what comes first? To be friends with Me or friends with My friends?"

There it was. That was what was wrong. I had been so busy being friends with Jesus' friends that I had left too little time to be friends with Jesus! Silly woman!

I made sure I redressed the balance – and then even the times with my friends were better. Be careful, it's a question of balance.

Lord, you are my dearest friend.

Don't let me ever forget it!

HARVEST TIME

God is never late and His clocks keep perfect time,
He works His works as he decides, in rhythm and in rhyme,
He plans each moment and each day and chooses us to go
Into a world that's spoiled by sin and tell them that He knows…

He knows the lives of men and sees the broken hearts and tears,
He grieves the harassed helpless crowds and mourns the wasted
    years,
He sends us to the harvest fields and tells us all to bring
A message of eternal life, and hear the Seraph sing…

So ordinary people who've had Christ forgive their sin
Are called to offer life and help – the power to begin
A life of precious joy and peace, and power to impart
The news of God the Spirit, who can fill the empty heart!

MY UNIFORM

"So [Jesus] got up from the meal, took off his outer
clothing, and wrapped a towel round his waist.
After that he poured water into a basin and began
to wash his disciples' feet, drying them with the towel
that was wrapped round him... When he had finished
washing their feet he [said]... 'Now that I, your
Lord and Teacher, have washed your feet, you
also should wash one another's feet!'"
John 13: 4–5, 12

We were on the outskirts of the Philippines visiting a
couple who were missionaries. We walked on Smokey Mountain,
a huge mountain of garbage, a smouldering rubbish heap on
which people actually live. Slum dwellings like this are among the
worst in the world. We walked down the putrid streets following
our friends who were talking to vendors and children, families
and "baggers".

I was aware Another walked with us, wanting to introduce
us to His "friends' friends" in this place.

"These missionaries belong to the Order of the Towel," He
said. "Both these young people, highly qualified in their

professions in your country, followed me here with their three young children to live near Smokey Mountain so they could wash feet. It's good you came to encourage them, it's not easy."

I watched the young mother greeting another young mother. Standing there with their arms around each other they were both Jesus-lovers and glory-givers. And they were from two different worlds, yet "not of this world" so the Golden Book says. They talked and then prayed, right there in the dirt and noise and commotion.

The missionary, her eyes shining, introduced us to her friend. Her compassion was tangible. The young husband was helping to catch a pig an elder of the church had lost. The "church" was right there in the very heart of the slum, next to the open sewer that floods over the ramshackle shacks whenever it rains (just like it was then!).

We sat down in the midst of it all, feeling loved and appreciated and welcomed by a room full of people for whom Christ had died, and for whom He had sent a young American family of servants – to love and nurture them.

That night, in our clean and tidy hotel room, I thought of Jesus stripping to the waist and washing His disciples' feet, and then I thought of our young friends and I was greatly humbled. I spent time in the Golden Book reading about Jesus in the upper room. After that I prayed, "O Lord, may I be known as they are known, by my uniform, the Towel!"

104

> I see You smiling while I strip my
>   clothes of comfort off,
> I hear You laugh as water splashes
>   in the bowl,
> I look above and catch Divinity's
>   Delight,
> I kneel and seek with washing word
>   to cleanse a soul
>
> Yet I could never dare to dress in
>   Servant's garb

Unless I first have known Your
    cleansing blood,
Have fallen prostrate, crying,
    "Mercy Lord…
Forgive my filthy feet their
    wayward road."

So humble this high head
    till low it bows,
Before the cross where sacred head
    hangs low.
Teach me the lowly secret of
    the Christ,
Then help me hear You say, "My servant – go."

SPENT

I sat still.
The Helper helped. The Father fathered me. Jesus was Jesus.
Glory!

THE GARDEN OF GRACE

FLAT CAMELS

THE ANGEL OF THE LORD TOUCHED HIM [ELIJAH] AND SAID,
"GET UP AND EAT FOR THE JOURNEY IS TOO MUCH FOR YOU."
I Kings 19:7

*E*LIJAH HAD RUN TILL HE WAS EXHAUSTED. Flat on his face under a broom tree he asked God to end his life. "I've had enough Lord," he said! The problem was that he was running on empty. Have you ever found yourself like Elijah? I have. God always meets his tired servants when they've run out. He cooks them breakfast – just as He did for Elijah. He knows how to replenish our soul.

What is going on in the Deep Place where nobody goes – in your heart?

Once I was struggling with the issue of spiritual burnout. I was involved in youth missions and it was tough. But I had been a youth worker for a few years and I had learned to play the game – smile the smile and look like a missionary, talk like a missionary and act like a missionary. The only thing I couldn't do with a degree of expertise was sing like a missionary!

I worked myself into the ground. I ran faster and faster till I ended up under the proverbial broom tree. My children began to play up. What is wrong with them? I grumbled. They were driving me crazy! They began to resent the mission, the missionaries and our whole lifestyle. When they whined I smiled a hard, brittle "Jesus smile" and told them it was a privilege to serve the Lord in a difficult situation.

But I soon saw that my children were not *creating* my attitude, they were simply *revealing* it! Kids are great at seeing the heart of the matter, and basically I had to admit that what was the matter with my heart was the heart of the matter!

I was running on empty. My inner life had atrophied. The joy had fled. The shadows wouldn't go away. All that was left was an unhappy, unthankful young woman whose heart was cold and who was running so hard – working her heart out for God – that she was out of energy, ideas, compassion for kids, and sleep!

Fortunately there were people I was accountable to who could see what was (or what *wasn't*) happening. They knew there was no smile on my heart even though there was a smile on my face. Some had had similar struggles and could read the signs. They loved me enough to see if they could help.

"I didn't think it showed," I muttered miserably.

"Well it does," they told me cheerfully. "You're a pretty good hypocrite, but we knew there was nothing going on down there inside of you because no one's been receiving anything from you for a while!" Ouch! That sent me to the Steps of my soul.

"It's true, Lord," I howled when He graciously came and sat on the Steps with me. "I'm empty! I've nothing left to give."

"It's been true for a long time," He agreed without any hint of condemnation. Then gently, "The journey is too much for you."

I realized then it had been too long since I had led anyone to Christ, been an encouragement to a friend, really prayed with my kids beyond the "Now I lay me down to sleep" thing, or revelled in God myself.

"I'm sorry," I said.

"We need to talk," He answered. And we did, till the shadows flew away and I was ready to walk out into the sunshine with the kiss of God on my face and, in truth and joy unspeakable and full of glory in my soul again.

"Maybe I need to stop running. All this activity – my Sunday school class, take a break from youth work – just stay home and regroup."

"You mean quit?" he asked mildly.

"No, but maybe I should stop running so fast and furious."

"You don't need to stop running," He replied, "though we can talk about prioritizing. I've wanted to help you with that but I haven't seen you in a while! You don't need to stop running, Jill, you need to stop *running on empty*!" Then we settled down to business.

As I was preparing to leave the Deep Place and return to the Shallow Place and start running again, I remembered a magazine article I had been reading about camels!

"I was reading this missionary newsletter, Lord…" (As if I had to tell Him. He gets all the missionary newsletters in the world and reads them all in an instant.) "You know, the one with a picture of a camel after a long drive across a desert," I continued. "It looked really funny and I couldn't figure out why. Then I realized it was running out of food."

"It had a flat hump?" He asked with a twinkle in His eye.

"Er, yes – it reminded me of me. I feel as if I've been running across a desert carrying this heavy load of work and now I've used up my store of food and feel like a flat camel!" Then we both laughed.

Before I left we read the Golden Book together and I began to replenish that "hump"! Soon I wouldn't be running on empty any more! Just like Elijah was replenished under his broom tree, I went 40 days and nights on the food He fed me from the Golden Book that day. And I didn't even realize I was running!

I have found that the devil never stops trying to get us running on empty one way or another. Don't let him do it to you! Go to the Deep Place inside you: you'll find Him waiting. He'll say to your soul, "the journey is too great for you, rest here awhile. Let me prepare some food for your soul. We'll eat it together."

THE GARDEN OF GRACE

COMING APART BEFORE
WE COME APART

"AND HE SAID UNTO THEM, 'COME YE YOURSELVES APART
INTO A DESERT PLACE, AND REST A WHILE,
FOR THERE WERE MANY COMING AND GOING,
AND THEY HAD NO LEISURE SO MUCH AS TO EAT."
Mark 6:31 KJV

———— ⟨⟩ ————

"*L*ORD," I SAID, "You were always loving, serving, touching and blessing, even when You were tired or discouraged. Today I feel all poured out. I can't face one more needy person and it's only 10am! I'm depleted, spent, down. Renew me, Lord."

We were taking meetings on Vancouver Island, Canada, in the beautiful mountains, and it had been non-stop since we arrived: speaking, teaching, listening, praying. The scenery was gorgeous, but we had been so busy we might as well have been in an underground shelter in central New York for all we had seen of our environment!

I thought about how in the midst of His incredible ministry Jesus would say to His disciples, "Come away and rest a while," and they would climb the hills above their beloved Sea of Galilee and be refreshed.

I knew He was saying, "Find me here, Jill. Just a step away from all your rushing about." He was saying as He said to His disciples, "Come ye apart and rest a while," (or *you* will come apart!).

So I stopped, right in the middle of a hectic morning, walked outside and found a robin singing about summer, a tiny flower with its head just above ground smiling at the song, and a soft breeze blowing.

"Lord, I'd forgotten how You gave us Your incredible creation to bless us. I see Your 'finger work' all around me. Thank you."

That afternoon, instead of going to one more meeting (where we didn't have to be), Stuart and I walked "our Galilee" together. My Stuart loves God's world. After God's breath of fresh air, back at our cabin at the conference, my husband caught the way that simple time in the woods renewed us both as we walked and worshipped together.

> Sunlight glancing through the trees,
> Branches dance to summer breeze,
> Eagles circle azure sky,
> Redwoods reaching up on high,
> Reminding me of You, Lord,
> Reminding me of You.

Warm as the sunlight,
Gentle as the breeze,
Vigilant as eagles,
Steadfast as the trees,
So are You to me, Lord,
So are You to me!

Take a walk outside, find a park, a pond, a walking track. Sit on a
hill or by a lake. Give yourself permission to "come apart" (before
you come apart) and worship. You won't be sorry!

HANGING UP YOUR HARP ON THE WEEPING WILLOW TREE

"By the rivers of Babylon, there we sat down, yea, we wept, when we remembered Zion."

Psalm 137:1 KJV

*H*AVE YOU LOST YOUR JOY? Do you feel it's been a long, long time since the Lord touched the heartstrings of your innermost being? On which tree have you hung up your joy? Is

it the Grief Tree? The Gripe Tree? The Grind Tree? Or even the Geriatric Tree? When did your heart last sing a song?

My heart had lost its song and therefore lost its strength – for "the joy of the Lord is my strength". I went to the Steps to see if I could find it again. He came near.

"I'm out of joy Lord," I began.

"So I see," He said. He had the Golden Book in His hands and was reading it. "This will remind you of the place where you lost it," He said handing me the Book.

He showed me the part in the Scriptures where the Babylonians were taunting the children of Israel who at that time were slaves. They were sitting besides the waters of Babylon weeping. They had hung up their harps on the weeping willow trees.

The Babylonians said to them, "Go on, sing us one of your merry little songs, one of the songs of Zion." The children of Israel replied bitterly, "How can we sing a song in a foreign land?"

"I can understand it, Lord," I said. "Who would feel like singing when they've seen babies murdered before their eyes and their parents chained to chariots and dragged through the streets or marched off to slavery. I'd be bitter. Who has any music left in him then?"

He was looking at me and I knew He wanted to talk about the place where I had hung up "my harp" and the song in my heart had been drowned in the river of bitterness.

"Lord, how can I sing when I have nothing to sing about?"

I asked silently. Like the children of Israel I'd never thought this would happen to me. This was a "foreign" experience – a strange place to be! As I sat with the Golden Book on my knee thinking about it, I realized that I, like the children of Israel, had a responsibility to sing a song to the Babylonians.

I read on in the presence of the Lord. (It always makes such a difference when you're conscious He is there reading along with you!) Back at the waters of Babylon, the taunts continued. And suddenly the Babylonians heard it. The sound of a harp. An old man with fire in his eyes was singing a song of Zion!

"Who was he, Lord?" I asked.

"One of the temple musicians," He said briefly. "It was a beautiful song – a song of comfort and hope for God's people in exile. I gave it to him."

I looked on the golden page then. The words read:

Comfort, comfort my people says your God…
Those who hope in the Lord will renew their strength.
They will soar on wings like eagles; they will run and not
grow weary, they will walk and not be faint.

From Isaiah 40

"O Lord," I said, "the Babylonians must never have heard such a beautiful song in all of their lives! It must have made them yearn for a song in the Deep Place that was song-less inside them because You had never visited their soul!"

Then He was gone for a little while and I knew He wanted me to wait on the Steps of my soul and compose a song. A song to my God, to His people and to my world that was "waiting for them to wait". I thought I heard Him say, "I'm so glad you came near. I was waiting for you so that they could be comforted." So on that particular joyless day I came.

The words came straight to my readied heart from the Golden Pages, and were followed by joy beams that wouldn't quit dancing around and singing my pain away!

> I Am Jehovah, the God of Eternity who created heaven
>   and earth, the God who doesn't wear out or decay.
> I am the Everlasting God – who lasts:
> The Powerful One – who is never powerless;
> The Changeless One – who doesn't change;
> The same great unwearied God, who never wearies;
> The strength of your life and days.

Later, I took down my harp from the weeping willow tree by my river of tears and offered my little prayer song in return.

> Joy of my joys,
> Light of my life,
> Strength in my weakness,
> Peace in my strife.
> Finding a song in my darkest of days,

Running on empty

Faith in my fearfulness,
Praise of my praise.

Spread help in my helplessness,
Quiet in my mind,
Save me from torment,
The "shame and guilt" kind.
Still me in stillness
Till I hardly dare breathe,
"Jesus! It's happening.
I really believe!"

Faith in my fearfulness,
Hope for despair,
Beauty for ashes,
Confidence rare.
As I wait in the Waiting Room
Under Your wings,
I'm filled with Your fullness
And ready to sing!

Can you join me in the chorus?

Waiting on God who is waiting for me,

My harp's in my hands and NOT on the tree!

Amen

Running on empty

ACROSS THE MILES

*T*WAS "HEART HUNGRY" for my grandchildren. We were staying in a missionary home with five beautiful children running all over the room and we loved it, but they weren't ours! You know what I mean. It just made the ache worse!

"I wish we could have our kids in the room with us." I said to Him.

"Come over to My House," He said. "You can meet in the Throne Room! Why don't you write and invite them?"

So I went Heart Deep – right then and there among all the noise and fun – and asked the Lord to help me write an email. It turned out to be pretty short when I finally got to my computer but when I'd finished, a poem began to spill onto the page. Sometimes it helps to say things in another way. This is what I wrote:

To our loved grandkids – Danny, Ty, Mike,
Christy, David, Drew, Brooke, Jordan, Stephen,
Cameron, Annika, Liam, Kendal.

Do you know how much Nana loves and misses
each one of you? When I pray for you across the miles
I put my arms around your heart. When we pray for each
other we kneel together in the Throne Room. There's
no space then – only togetherness! Think about that
next time you pray. I wrote a poem about it.

Love Nana

xxxxxxxxxxxxx (13 kisses!)

Across the miles – I live across the miles
From those I love, their touch, their loving smiles.
Across the miles so far from comforts there
That others take for granted unaware
That some for love of Him and for His sake
Must live across the miles and home forsake.

We two are two who chose to follow Him
And take the gospel where it's never been –
The distance like a chasm none can leap.
We ache in humid nights when none can sleep,
What miracle that birthed our grandkids rare,
Across the miles you reach us with your prayer.

Across the miles, we seem so far apart,
I'm missing all those hugs that melt my heart.
Across the miles the pain is no less real,
Across the miles the loneliness I feel.
These miles – no miles to Him who spans the globe,
For Him who sits in heaven's Glory robe.

You children big and small, though strong or weak,
Your prayers reach out and kiss me on the cheek!
Across the miles I love and you love me,
No chasm large can stop you reaching me!
So come, let's talk a while where'er we are
'Tis Him who brings us near though we be far.

So on our knees we'll meet in Throne Room high,
To laugh and play and touch and feel and cry.
O Lord we love you so, what joy is here,
Across the miles in prayer when we draw near.

Across the miles we
        closer still can be
Than home within the
        same vicinity.

So come, let's talk awhile
        where'er we are
Through Him who
        brings us near
        though we be far
So know, my loves, each
        one a precious piece
Of who I am, till life on
        earth shall cease.
Across the miles as we
        spend time apart,
Across the miles you're
        living in my heart!

All my love, Nana.
March 2005

THE LOCK BOX

═══════════ ⟨ᴑ⟩ ═══════════

*S*TUART WAS DRIVING ME DOWN to the airport in Milwaukee to go to Dallas. In the usual pre-flight rush I stuffed some mail and a jar of honey I had been given for our family into my carry-on bag. I meant to leave the honey at church on the way to my flight but I forgot. Then I forgot that I'd forgotten the honey. I boarded the plane to Dallas/Fort Worth (DFW), never suspecting that by the time I got off the flight the honey would have exploded and coated *everything* in my carry-on bag! I had taken my computer out of the big computer bag as it was a small plane and I wanted to put the larger bag in the hold. In the pocket of the small computer bag I took on board with me were three printed chapters of a book I was writing on Ecclesiastes that I wanted to edit on the journey.

Unaware of the sticky mess under my seat, I gathered my things together as we landed at DFW and opened my carry-on to get out the information I needed to meet up with the people taking me to Tyler, Texas for my first meeting. UGH!

I made a beeline for the Ladies and began furiously washing off what I could of the honey and stuffing paper towels in the sticky mess that was left, wondering if the people were still

_126_

waiting for their guest speaker to turn up. I did the best I could and ran down the escalator to the baggage claim area; not realizing in my haste I had left my computer on the washbasin!

I didn't find that out till I arrived in Tyler, Texas – DFW was two hours away! Fred my gracious host, looking at my horrified face, simply said, "You've come here to talk about 'Prayer That Works', Jill. Let's do it!" and then prayed for my lost computer – with so much writing and sermons and work (not all backed up) recorded in its clever little mind (however that works).

Thus began three days of ministry punctuated with frantic calls to DFW that proved fruitless and frustrating. We discovered that lost items from my terminal were put in a lock box (a locker) on the concourse. Then they were sent to another terminal to another "Lost and Found", but not until Friday! (I had arrived on Sunday.) I couldn't get a real live person to go and unlock the box and look inside! Between teachings from Philippians about how to overcome worry, rejoice in trouble and enjoy the peace that passed understanding. I called every security guard I could get hold of at DFW – or so it seemed – to no avail!

When we eventually got hold of a real live person, we were told the famous lock box that just "might" contain my precious computer was the other side of the airport from the "Lost and Found" place we were talking to! There was no thought of *them* going to look for us.

"It's all the way over the other side of the airport," they informed us with hurt in their voices.

"Get the train," I wanted to shout into the phone – "like we passengers do!" There was nothing to do but continue to preach on "patience and forbearance" to hundreds of ladies who seemed to be perfectly patient and forbearing (unlike me), and wait till I left Dallas.

The morning my patient daughter-in-law who lives in Dallas took me to the airport, we left an hour earlier than the early arrival time required, so I could go in person to ALL the Lost and Founds and assorted lock boxes at DFW. As Libby drove me hither and yon, and after a hurried and fruitless search with my eye on the clock, I tracked down the famous lock box by Gate 1 where I had come in and where I was leaving. I gazed hungrily at the padlock! However, I now had only twenty minutes to get on the plane. I looked at the gate thinking I would beg the girl to hold the plane and open the box or find someone who had been trained to do this (how hard can it be?) and saw there was no one at the desk. Then I looked at the monitor and discovered they had changed the gate for my plane from number 1 to number 10! I now had fifteen minutes before the flight left.

I hared (or rather lumbered) down the corridor, like a plane that was too old and too heavy to get off the ground, and arrived at Gate 10.

"You're out of breath," one of the desk people said accusingly!

I spluttered, "Well, I lost my computer on Sunday and I have been looking on every wing of this airport – and didn't have a chance to look in the lock box by the gate I arrived at – because you changed the gate to number 10!"

"What is your computer like?" asked the other agent.

"It's a Compaq."

"Name on it?"

"No," I said, "but there is a file in the pocket with "Ecclesiastes" written on it." Seeing the blank faces I muttered, "It's a book in the Bible –"

"I have your computer." said the agent! "It's in my personal locker." I was struck dumb. "It was brought to me on Sunday night," she said. "I couldn't find a name on it, but I looked in the file in the pocket and said to my friend 'This person is writing about God! This is an important computer – I must find the person.'"

For two days this woman had tried to trace me through old Delta tickets she found stuffed in the pocket of the computer from previous flights. She got a phone number from Delta and tried to phone my home but the number wasn't right and she got no reply!

"Why didn't you put it in the lock box?" I asked, clutching my computer moments later.

"They only pick it up on Fridays," she answered, "and I didn't want to chance leaving it there."

I thanked her, making little appreciative sounds, gushing

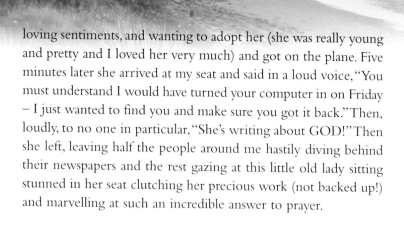

loving sentiments, and wanting to adopt her (she was really young and pretty and I loved her very much) and got on the plane. Five minutes later she arrived at my seat and said in a loud voice, "You must understand I would have turned your computer in on Friday – I just wanted to find you and make sure you got it back." Then, loudly, to no one in particular, "She's writing about GOD!" Then she left, leaving half the people around me hastily diving behind their newspapers and the rest gazing at this little old lady sitting stunned in her seat clutching her precious work (not backed up!) and marvelling at such an incredible answer to prayer.

Later that night, breathless on the Steps, I asked the Lord to forgive my irresponsibility.

"Lord, You take such good care of me! You answer prayers I neither deserve nor have earned. It's all grace! It amazes me that You go to such lengths to turn my failings into blessing for others. Thank You."

I sat there quietly in the clear air thinking about the three chapters of Ecclesiastes read by people who perhaps would never know about the wonderful words of Solomon, who found purpose and meaning not in wealth and riches but in fearing the Living God. I thought too of how God hates losing things that are precious to Him, and understands when we lose things that are precious to us.

He spoke then, reminding me that God is a seeking and finding God. And I told Him I am so encouraged by His care for the details of my life and how thankful I am that He answers the cries of His children and turns them to other people's good.

"Forgive me, Lord, help me to be a whole lot more responsible than I am!" I asked.

"All right. You need to focus on the matter at hand," He said.

"Like the computer? Sorry!"

A few days later, I went to pack my bags for yet another trip. After a while it was time to leave for the airport. Now, where had I put my Bible – and my keys?

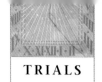

TIME

I KNEW WHEN HE CAME. Time stood still. He always does when we are there in the Deep Place – he doesn't want to distract! Time waited for us to talk. He doesn't mind waiting. He knows his days are numbered – and when "Time's time" has come he will be changed into eternity.

Till then, Time loves watching Him work His works in the hearts of men. That is what Time is for! Time loves hanging around – it makes him feel needed. He knows it takes the power of God to change a life, but he also knows he can help – because it takes Time!

Lord, I know Time is a great healer but, of course, it's

You who heals – Time just helps. Help me be patient

and let You do your work – in Your good Time!

Amen

TRIALS

Help me accept the trials allowed –
My losses and my troubles.
Help me accept that life is not
A pretty bowl of bubbles.
May I remember there's no
Empty tomb without a tree,
That Jesus wouldn't save Himself,
But died to set me free.

Help me when crying on my bed
To know – You count my tears,
Have planned my moments and my days
And brooded o'er my years.
And so I ask your help, dear God,
To bear the pain life gives,
Endure with joy my darkest hour,
For my Redeemer lives.

Trials

A CAN OF WORMS

"…THAT THEY MAY HAVE THE FULL RICHES OF COMPLETE
UNDERSTANDING, IN ORDER THAT THEY MAY KNOW THE
MYSTERY OF GOD, NAMELY, CHRIST, IN WHOM ARE HIDDEN ALL
THE TREASURES OF WISDOM AND KNOWLEDGE."
Colossians 2:2b–3

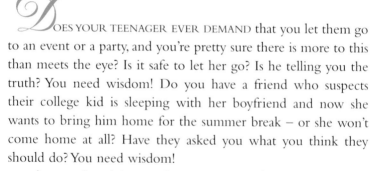

134

DOES YOUR TEENAGER EVER DEMAND that you let them go to an event or a party, and you're pretty sure there is more to this than meets the eye? Is it safe to let her go? Is he telling you the truth? You need wisdom! Do you have a friend who suspects their college kid is sleeping with her boyfriend and now she wants to bring him home for the summer break – or she won't come home at all? Have they asked you what you think they should do? You need wisdom!

Are you in ministry and your youngster has just announced they aren't going to the church youth group or, for that matter, to church any more – it's boring! (Cardinal sin!) Or has your young adult told you he has become an adherent to another faith? Do you have a dilemma over an elderly parent and their care? Did your sister's child announce she was gay and ask to talk to her favourite aunt or uncle – you? Who is sufficient for these things? I'm not!

Who will judge wisely and well and find just the right words to change a mind, halt a proposed disastrous course of action, find a third way in an impasse or a radical solution that is acceptable to all in a church fight? Are you the one who comes up with a brilliant strategy that will cool hot heads and bring reason to bear? When David's son Solomon asked for wisdom to judge a very difficult case, guess who he asked for help from? That's right, the Father, "the only wise God." Years ago, in the face of life's conundrums, I decided to do the same!

I had been asked for help by two church families. I needed a lot of wisdom. The situation was so complicated. In fact it was "a can of worms".

"Why ask me?" I asked the Lord petulantly! "Just because my husband is the Pastor they expect me to know all the answers! I hate worms! You know, Lord, I'm not a confronter!" Then accusingly, "You didn't make me a psychologist! I don't need this!" By now I was having a spiritual tantrum.

There was no answer from Him, so I sat on the Steps and sulked. Why be dragged into this unpleasant mess? I knew from experience I would end up getting shot at from both sides. I was tempted to open up the can and throw the worms to the birds and suggest the warring groups went into group therapy, or read a book on resolving conflict (there were plenty out there by the experts), or they could go to another church if they didn't like ours! That sounded the best option to me. But of course I couldn't do that. He was watching to see what I would do. So, presumably, were the "so great a cloud of witnesses". Embarrassing!

So I made a list of all the "land mines" facing me in this situation. It was a long list, in fact, I was still adding to it when He came, sat down, took my list into His hands and handed me the Golden Book instead.

"You can't turn the pages of the Golden Book when your hands are full of your lists of problems, Jill," He said mildly. He turned to the concordance at the back of my Bible and suggested I looked up the word "wisdom". I did. It was rich. This exercise gave me all sorts of wisdom about wisdom! I would look up a reference and tell Him something I had learned from it in my own words. Then we would talk about it.

"Write it down," He said.

"Lord, after reading some of these verses, I'm thinking that, 'wisdom' is spiritual intelligence. Right?"

"That's part of it," He said.

"So, I can't be wise without 'The Spirit of Wisdom?'"

"That's obvious," He replied.

I didn't like to mention that it hadn't been obvious to me! I had believed there was other wisdom to be had – worldly wisdom. And then there was the wisdom of the aged. Of course, it is said that "there's no fool like an old fool", but experience of life has to count for something!

He interrupted my thinking with "The word 'wisdom' really means 'life skill'. Wisdom is 'spiritual intelligence': practical God-solutions for life's insolubles."

So I couldn't be wise without God! Well I knew that, but you sort of forget when you learn a skill and you think (secretly, of course) that you are highly trained, educated or successful at it. Like teaching. Even teaching the Bible. Pride is a lethal thing. That's where the whole mess started in the first place! With the devil persuading Adam and Eve to be their own wisdom-makers and do without the wisdom given by walking with God in the cool of the day, instead using their own (inference "superior") wisdom to figure out life lived on earth.

I thought about my teaching and how I would say (humbly, of course) to any who complimented me, "Thank you, you are so kind, the Lord helped me." And I wondered, uncomfortably, if I had learned the teaching skill so well that that was just lip service in the end, and I had no idea if I was dependent on Him for the words or not!

As my mind was busy with this He handed me a quote from some really awesome biblical teacher that I had heard of by reputation.

"Interesting," He commented. I read it. Interesting? It was shattering!

It said: "It is possible to be homiletically brilliant, verbally fluent, theologically profound, Biblically accurate and orthodox and *spiritually useless!*" That frightens me. I hope it frightens you!

And continued: "It is very easy for us to be so concerned about homiletical ability and fluency, and theological profundity and biblical accuracy, but for God to say, "Preach on great Preacher – *without Me*."

Could I teach on without Him? Could I count myself like Eve to be Mrs God all on my little own? Had I come to instruct and give words of counsel while relying on my gathered knowledge – even in the very act of teaching the Golden Book or giving sage advise to a hurting person – just because I had done it before so many times I almost knew the message off by heart?

"Yes," He said! "You could."

Oh, my!

"That's just imparting knowledge then, Lord. That's not giving wise words that will work in a supernatural way."

"Knowledge is knowledge. It takes spiritual insight and power, added to experience in life skill to impart knowledge on My behalf for their greater good and blessing."

Humbled greatly I asked, "How do I get to be so wise?" He didn't answer because He didn't have to. I knew. (Why do I ask Him things I know the answer to?) I must spend much time with the only wise God. The more time I spent on the Steps of my soul reading the Golden Book and talking about it with Him, the better and wiser servant I would be, and the more that "given wisdom" would be sought by others.

For the next year I studied the wonderful wisdom books

most believe were written by Solomon, the wisest man on earth. (Though who could really consider him wise when he said "I do" a thousand times!) "That part of his history was when he chose to play the fool instead of choosing to be wise," the Lord commented one day. "The Father told him not to multiply gold, horses or women and he multiplied all three. In the end his wives stole away his heart from the Lord God. He never said no to himself! Choose wisdom, Jill, choose wisdom."

After that day we had a wonderful time on the Steps. He pointed out the points in the pages of Ecclesiastes, lighting up the text as only He can. And in the end He helped me write "a book about the book" and all I had learned of the wisdom of God and obedience to it, which is "the whole duty of man".

There is no short cut to being a wise woman. I must soak in the wisdom of the Word, and then I will know what to do "can of worms by can of worms!" No amount of "human" wisdom can figure it out!

Wisdom

A PRAYER FOR WISDOM

O Lord God, great Shepherd of Israel,

Give me a wise, discerning mind
To judge the hardest cause,
Give me a prudent, knowing heart,
A copy Lord of Yours.

As I spend time "Heart Deep" with You
About the human race,
Give me some light to see what's right,
Reflected in Your face!

May wisdom's words be on my tongue,
May life skill be at hand,
The words I use – the heat diffuse,
As I perceive Your plan.

Christ is my wisdom, He's my truth,
My counsel, teacher, friend,
Make me a wise, obedient child,
The trusted one to send.

O Shepherd, as I wait on Thee,
Give me the word to know
How the weak to strengthen,
Strong inspire,
The frantic quiet and slow!

Here am I – send me!
Amen

Not only was the Teacher wise, but also he imparted knowledge to the people. He pondered and searched out and set in order many proverbs. The Teacher searched to find just the right words, and what he wrote was upright and true.
The words of the wise are like goads, their collected sayings like firmly embedded nails — given by one Shepherd. Be warned, my son, of anything in addition to them.

Ecclesiastes 12:9–12

A GRATITUDE ATTITUDE

"...GIVE THANKS IN ALL CIRCUMSTANCES, FOR THIS IS GOD'S
WILL FOR YOU IN CHRIST JESUS."
1 Thessalonians 5:18

I WOKE GRATEFUL. It doesn't often happen. I usually wake worried, gripped by a sense of "something bad is going to happen to me"! Fear usually pervades my waking moments! I went "Heart Deep" to talk to the Lord about this.

"It happened. I did what You said and I woke grateful!"

He smiled.

"I've got so I don't want to wake up! I'm gripped by dread before my feet touch the floor!"

"Try asking Me to give you your waking thought," He said. "As soon as you come out of sleep turn your thoughts heavenward. Ask Me for that gift of grace."

"I'll try." Then, "How will I know it's a thought You are giving me?"

"It will be something to be thankful for. Gratitude is the

language of worship. It sets your sails for the day, carries you through it and brings you into safe harbour at night."

"Gratitude?"

"Gratitude."

"Stuart talks a lot about the 'Gratitude Attitude' and lives with one! I wish I could. He wakes up positive; I wake up negative."

"Ask Me." He said

"OK."

So I started trying to do that. It was hard. But it worked! Try it! I stayed a while in the Deep Place to pen some words about the new spiritual skill I was learning. I decided I had a choice. To be gripped by an unreasonable and debilitating fear or to be gripped by Grace. No contest!

Waking each morning glancing above,
Determined to think of His marvellous love.
Struggling to thank Him for all He has done,
Believing He'll help me the hard race to run,
Learning to praise as I wake in the dawn,
Finding relief and sweet peace in the morn.

Gripped by the Godhead, grasping His grace,
Gratitude showing all over the place,
Being obedient to all that He says,
Working my heart out all of my days.
He gives me the tools and a measure of power
Moment by moment, each day and each hour.
Grace so amazing making me whole,
A gratitude attitude deep in my soul!

Gripped by the Godhead, and grasping His love,
Hemmed in to holiness, looking above.
Driven, directed and sent with His word
Out to the wide world where they've never heard
Love so amazing, love so complete,
What more could I do than fall down at His feet?

Gripped by a calling, elated I sing –
Jesus proclaiming as Saviour and King.
Reaching the heights for a God I adore,
Graced and endowed, could I want one thing more?
God so amazing, sharing with me,
Grace, love and mercy for eternity.

HEART SICK

HAVE YOU EVER BEEN in inner turmoil about something that happened to you long ago? Hurts in the past can hobble us in the present and crush our spirit. Does it make you "heartsick" thinking about it? I understand.

I had been reminded by the devil of an incident in the UK before I was married! Yes, years ago. A close friend and fellow Christian – one whom I looked up to and worked closely with – had used me for their own ends. It ended up torpedoing our close relationship.

I mean, come on! How could these memories rise unbidden again – after years and years – causing this sick feeling in my stomach? I thought that was all settled and I had let it go. But the memories surfaced, triggered by another very similar situation a friend was going through, and pictures of that incident danced around my mind and crushed my heart all over again! I needed to have some time on the Steps of my soul.

Sitting on the Steps I looked around but there was no sign

of Him. It happens sometimes. I was a little impatient. Here I was, heart sick and needing Him to jump to it and heal my heart! So why didn't He come running? I thought the thought as quietly as I could in case He heard it, and asked myself petulantly why it was taking Him so long to come. I mean when you're heart sick all you want is someone to tuck you into bed, kiss you goodnight and give you a heavenly aspirin – extended relief!.

I began to put in time thinking about my malady. I admitted it was a chronic complaint that had needed attention ages ago instead of me settling for Band Aids. I began to play with words on paper to pass the time. Anyway, it was a good idea to write it out first – to clarify things before I talked it out with Him when He came.

Since talking to my friend about her similar experience it had been hard to concentrate on the present moment, once my own pain had surfaced. I played the "I should have" game for a while, then "she should have" for some more minutes, then "God should have", and then gave up that fruitless exercise and wondered why something over thirty years ago seemed to me to have happened just yesterday! I realized I had never really left it behind.

It took a while to choose all the words that described my problem, but at last it was done. It turned into a poem about getting "past the past".

I cannot get past the past, Lord,
I cannot undo what was said.

I think I'm depressed
Though my part is confessed
And I don't want to get out of bed.

I cannot live well in the present
While so angry, hurt and confused,
So I'm coming to You
To know what I should do
When remembering how I've been used.

I cannot look out at the future,
When I cannot move on from the past,
I'm so near to tears
And obsessed by my fears
That no good intentions will last.

So I'm stuck here in sad desperation,
I can't even think of a prayer.
I'm tired with trying
And sobbing and crying:
"The whole thing just wasn't fair!"

The words dried up. I sat still, very still, realizing it was just as if the whole horrible row was playing out all over again in glorious technicolour right then and there! How could something so "past" be so "present"? I couldn't make up any more words to describe it; I couldn't "give the whole thing to Him" all over again, though sitting there on the Steps of my soul I tried so very hard to do so! It sort of stuck to my soul like Velcro and wouldn't go! In the end I came to the end of myself, and just gave up.

"Lord," I said, "I give You permission to take it."

I have no idea how many minutes passed, or it could even have been an hour, but when I stopped trying to get relief – the relief came! Once more, my hand reached for the pencil and paper and I finished my poem.

As soon as I came to the end of myself
And asked Him to heal poor old me,
When I gave Him permission,
I went into remission –
And now I'm as well as can be!

Then I realized He had been there all the time, but my striving had been so intense I hadn't seen Him there – just waiting for me to stop trying to exert faith and heal myself!

Try it! Stop striving to "cast your burden" when it won't be cast! Just say:

> *Lord, I can't twist Your arm, I can't shout loud enough for You to hear my voice in heaven, and I can't cry hard enough to ensure You'll come running. Help, I'm through trying to get freedom from this thing by my own "faith effort" or my own anything. You do it, Lord. Heal my memories. Heal my heart. Amen*

Then stay there doing NOTHING till peace comes and the turmoil is gone.

THE GARDEN OF GRACE

THE THIEF

"CAST YOUR BURDEN UPON THE LORD,
AND HE SHALL SUSTAIN THEE."
Psalm 55:22 KJV

I CAME INTO THE THRONE ROOM with Jesus. The Father was on His throne. Of course, where else would He be? I had brought along a big weight of worry I had been carrying around for a long time. A parcel of pain I had become attached to in a funny sort of way. I had been carrying it all over the place for so long it had become like my American Express card. You know, a "Don't leave home without it!" thing. So I had lugged it along with me.

"Father Dear," I began, "I have this big bundle of pain about —" well then, I knew He knew what it was about, so I just stood there with the bundle held against my chest. I felt it pressing on my heart so it was hard to breath.

"In Jesus' name," I began again, glancing at the Lord who had come into the Throne Room with me and stood by my side. (You can't go there without Him you know).

Before I could get anything else out of my mouth He spoke – it was a sound like a waterfall falling all the way from heaven to earth. Even in the tumult of the waters I heard Him clearly. "Put it down. Let us talk of other things."

I couldn't remember the last time I had been in the Throne Room and talked of other things. And the truth of it was I didn't *want* to talk of "other" things! This burden was so absorbing and so overwhelming I couldn't wait till I'd told Him all about it for the umpteenth time!

"Put it down," He said again. So I gently laid it on the floor and took my hands off it. Oh my! That felt so good. Scary, but good!

I stayed a while and found myself talking of other things. The people Stuart and I had just been with in a country where Jesus' followers had to meet in secret and sing their hymns and songs in whispers in case they were heard. We talked about the unbelievable joy on their faces, and how they shared how glad they were for each other, and how they loved their enemies and prayed for those who hurt them.

"Father, help my friends in the

shadow of all this evil and lift the burden of the restrictions they have on their lives because they are believers." I asked.

We talked about our friends for a long time and I suddenly realized I was talking to the Father about "their burdens" and there had been no room in my tiny little mind for talk of mine! In fact, I'd actually forgotten about it for the first time in ages.

"I have your friends' problems in hand," He said, reading my thoughts, and I couldn't think of anyone's hands that were more suitable to carry my friends' troubles. And then I thrilled to the thought that I had been able to pick up their parcels of pain and put them into the Father's care.

"Champion their cause, Father," I asked and then added hastily, "In Jesus' Name. For His sake." I left.

As soon as I got outside the Front Door I missed the weight I had been carrying. I realized I had forgotten to pick up my big load again. I felt sort of insecure as I had been carting the thing around for so long, and wondered how I could manage without it. I began to panic. Maybe I was meant to carry the burden – like my friends we had been discussing in faraway places who were permitted to carry their burdens. Maybe if I didn't carry the thing I wouldn't pray as hard – or I might even forget to pray at all!

I couldn't see the Lord Jesus and presumed He had gone to look after the Father's business – He loves to do that – and so, glancing around and seeing no one, though I did hear something that sounded like wind, I slipped back inside the Throne Room. You have to use His name – it's the only way to enter – so I said to no one I could see, "In Jesus' Name, I come."

I couldn't see anything this time, but there was a mist singing beautiful music that bathed the room. (No, I can't tell you how a mist can sing, but this one did!) I looked around as best as I could and, though it was smoky, there was my bundle, lying just where I'd left it on the floor of the Throne Room.

I wondered if the angels were watching. (They have eyes all over them you know, so it's pretty impossible for them not to see you all the time.) But I couldn't see them so I hoped they would be on lunch break or something. I hurriedly bent down and picked up my parcel and ran out of the Front Door.

Whew! That felt better. Now I was weighed down again just like I was used to – and though the familiar heaviness slowed my steps and absorbed me again making me pretty miserable, it was a misery like an old grumpy friend. It felt "normal" to have him along again, spoiling my day. What's more, I felt more in control. I had my burden back! Suddenly a familiar shape appeared ahead of me. It was Jesus.

"Why did you do that?" He asked me.

Bother!

"Well, I thought it was giving up – just dumping it in front of the Father. He has enough burdens to bear without adding to them." I answered quite self-righteously, as if I had done something really grand. Then lightly, "I was tidying up the Throne Room floor room so no one tripped over my burden!"

"Jill," He answered, ignoring my silliness. "Do you think you can take care of this better than the Father can?" Then I heard words from the Golden Book being sung from a high place: "Cast your burden on the Lord, and He will sustain you."

"Do you want the Father to take care of this for you or do you want to take care of it for Him?" He asked me quite sternly. Well that was no contest! I hate hard choices, but this one was a "no-brainer". He gently turned me around and led me back the way I had come.

Oh dear, I thought. What will He say to me – when He knows?

Well that was pretty silly too. Of course He knew. If He who lives with the praise of angels, even though there is all that wonderful Glory Smoke in the Throne Room, hadn't seen me, He wouldn't be God! Of course I had been seen clearly through the mists of Majesty, scooping my parcel of pain into my arms again. How could I have imagined otherwise?

This time I found myself standing really close to the Throne. Of course, if Jesus hadn't been holding my arms to help me carry the weight, I could not have stood that near the power of all that Glory.

"Father Dear," I began, "I came back and –"

"I saw you," He replied. I couldn't see His face, but the voice was smiling!

Whew! That was good. But as I stood there I suddenly realized what I had done. I had taken something that was His! I had given it to God and then had stolen it back. I was a thief! How awful!

I began to put the bundle on the floor in front of Him again, feeling like the robber I was – and feeling awful about it all – but He said, "No, put it into my hands!" I knew if I did that I could not sneak back a second time and take it out of them, so I hesitated.

I had no notion that this burden had become so attached to me and I to it. Or how I had become so dependent on it. It wasn't that I liked the weight crushing my heart; it was a fear that if I put it in His hands I would be released from worrying and praying about it and then what would I do with my life? I would lose control. After all, I had been obsessed with the worry and the weight for a long time.

Standing there I realized something else. This pain had so absorbed me that I couldn't carry anything else for anyone – as my arms were already full and my hands occupied! But if I put it in His hands I could not take it back and it might wait for His time to get fixed. If I kept it in mine I might fix it sooner. (How stupid was that?)

"Put it in My hands, Jill. Then I know you will not come and try to take it back."

"It's called 'trust'," said Jesus quietly at my side.

Again I marvelled that I could hear Him above the incredible spiritual symphony that was going on in all my senses. So, at last, I took a deep breath, lifted my burden one more time and put it in His hands – in my Father's hands.

Back in the shallow places where everyone lives I noticed a difference. It didn't mean, I discovered, that I stopped praying –

and weeping – about it. But when I did, I thought about where the parcel of pain lay and knew He had promised to work in it for me.

After a few days, I noticed my hands could receive other work that they had been too full to grasp before. And when I was tempted to panic about the thing, I shut my eyes wherever I was and thought of the Throne Room and the Golden Words, and my Father's hands working on my parcel – untying the string, undoing the wrapping and dealing with it – piece by piece – and my heart went quiet and the weeping stopped and I rested inside!

What are you carrying around? Are you tired out? Worn down? Does the weight get weightier? The parcel heavier? Why not ask Jesus to take you into the Throne Room? He loves to be asked to help. Jesus will go with you and help you put your burden into the Father's hands. Leave it there. Don't be a thief!

Lord, I come to Your Throne Room because of
Jesus. I bear this burden of pain. It is too
heavy for Your child to carry but I try. I can't
carry it any more. I put my trouble in Your
"Father hands". Carry it for me, Father Dear,
carry it for me. Deal with it for me.
I will not come this way again to take it back,
I promise. Now fill my empty hands with Your
Things – for I would, like Your Son, "be about
my Father's business". Thank you!
In His Name that is above every name.

Amen

Jill Briscoe and her husband Stuart live in
Milwaukee, Wisconsin. They have worked
together for over 40 years, and have three
grown children and thirteen grandchildren.
A native of Liverpool, Jill is a prolific writer.
She serves on the board of directors of
World Relief and of *Christianity Today*, and is
a popular speaker at key Christian events
around the world.